Just a Very Pretty Girl from the Country :

SYLVIA SALINGER'S LETTERS FROM FRANCE 1912–1913

Edited with Foreword and Afterword by

Albert S. Bennett

Southern Illinois University Press
Carbondale and Edwardsville

For Dick
who shared the experience

Printed in the United States of America
Edited by Curtis L. Clark
Designed by Cindy Small
Production supervised by Natalia Nadraga

Library of Congress Cataloging-in-Publication Data
Salinger, Sylvia.
    Just a very pretty girl from the country.
    Includes index.
    1. Salinger, Sylvia—Correspondence.   2. Salinger, Sylvia—
Journeys—France.   3. United States—Biography.
4. Americans—France—Correspondence.
5. Americans—France—Paris—Intellectual life—
Sources.   I. Bennett, Albert S., 1925–   .   II. Title.
CT275.S3115A4   1987   944.081'3'0924   86-20218
ISBN 0-8093-1329-4

The paper used in this publication meets the minimum requirements of
American National Standard for Information Sciences
– Permanence of Paper for Printed Library Materials, ANSI Z39.48-1984.

Frontispiece: Sylvia Salinger (*right*) and her aunt Harriet Levy in
their *apartement*, 31 rue de Vaugirard, Paris

I don't see what all the fuss is about. Sylvia is just a very pretty girl from the country.

Gertrude Stein

CONTENTS

ILLUSTRATIONS

FOREWORD

We were a couple of lucky kids, my brother and I. We grew up in a house filled with the finest in music and art, thanks to a legacy of good taste handed down from Great-Grandfather to Grandmother to Mother. For example, over Mother's bed hung a group of small black-and-white reproductions of paintings by the French masters—Matisse, Picasso, Renoir, Degas—selected for her by Michael Stein from his collection and that of his sister Gertrude.

When Mother, Sylvia Salinger Bennett, died a few years ago at the age of ninety-four, we found among her papers an old stationery box filled with letters, postcards, and snapshots. These were the treasured mementos of her 1912–1913 sojourn in France. Mother, naive and sheltered at twenty-four, had been shipped off to Europe in the company of a maiden aunt because she had fallen in love with the boy next door. According to Sylvia's mother (my Grandmother Salinger), the Coffee boy—although he was Jewish and had a high-school-teacher father—was simply not quite good enough.

The story behind the letters really begins in the 1840s, when Benjamin Levy and Henriette Michelson both left their tiny villages in East Prussia. They reached San Francisco sometime around 1850, she via sailing vessel around Cape Horn, he by mule train across the Isthmus of Panama. Benish Levy prospered, outfitting the ships that plied the busy harbor and the miners who sought the gold of the Sierra Nevada. Benish and Yetta were married in 1858. They produced three daughters: Addie, my grandmother; Polly, later Mrs. Frank P. Jacobs; and Hattie, who was eventually well known as Harriet Lane Levy, author and art collector.

In 1874 Albert Salinger, then nineteen, arrived in California; he had been born at sea while his parents, too, were emigrating from Germany. After a year's apprenticeship at Samuels' Lace House, one of San Francisco's finer dry goods emporia, Albert moved across the bay to Oakland. In 1875 he opened the young city's first department store. Salinger's prospered, too, and in 1883 Albert won the hand of the Levy's first daughter. Addie Levy Salinger bore five children. Ruth, the oldest, was an accomplished violinist who married a brilliant young lawyer named Charles De Young ("Chip") Elkus; by 1912 they were living in San Francisco and had three children of their own. But the Salinger house at 911 Filbert Street in West Oakland was still filled with people. All three of the Salinger boys (Jeffrey, known as Jimmy; Herbert; and Robert, known as Babe) lived there, as did Grandma Levy (Grandpa had died in 1900); Grandma's companion, a Mrs. Peabody; and Albert Salinger's widowed sister Lena Sickles (who was to live with the Salingers, all expenses paid, for more than forty years). Sylvia was the Salingers' middle child, pretty and vivacious and indulged, a talented pianist and horsewoman, a swimming instructor and an avid student of the Montessori method of pedagogy.

In 1907, five years before Sylvia was to be shipped off to France, her aunt Harriet Levy had made the same trip, accompanied by her next-door neighbor and favorite traveling companion, Alice Toklas. In Paris Harriet renewed her acquaintance with the Stein family, all of whom she had known in California. There were Michael Stein, his wife,

Sarah, and their young son, Allan; there was Mike's younger brother, Leo; and there was their baby sister, Gertrude. Alice Toklas and Gertrude Stein fell in love; Harriet eventually returned to California alone—minus the $1,000 loan that had enabled Alice to finance her own trip ($1,000, by the way, that never was repaid).

So in 1912 Addie Levy Salinger decreed that the beauteous Sylvia was to be separated from the boy next door and to voyage abroad, chaperoned by her forty-six-year-old maiden aunt Harriet. A dutiful daughter, Sylvia went. And she requested that the family save all her letters home. Fortunately for us, they complied with her request. I have edited Mother's letters, but only to remove her frequent pleas for mail, some references to inconsequential family matters, and some proselytizing for Christian Science. The spelling and the punctuation—some of it remarkably creative (and frequently inconsistent)—are hers. Several pertinent letters from Harriet are included, as well as one from Sarah Stein. I have followed the writers' spelling and punctuation in these letters also. All of the photographs were taken by Michael Stein, except plates 6, 7, and 15 (I have been unable to determine the source or sources of these three photographs).

One further explanatory note: Sarah Samuels Stein, a Christian Science practitioner, had interested Harriet Levy in her faith. (Mrs. Stein was a bulwark of the little Second Church of Christ, Scientist, on the Left Bank, where services were held in both French and English.) Harriet, always eager to explore new intellectual and spiritual paths, was fascinated; she succeeded in converting nearly all of the Oakland Salingers. However, my mother and the Widow Sickles, my Great-Aunt Lena, were the only family members who maintained lifelong faith in Mary Baker Eddy's teachings. The positive thinking of Christian Science is one reason for the almost total lack of mention of negative events—and of the psychological distress caused by Sylvia's removal from her suitor—in the letters that follow. Another reason is that according to family tradition Sylvia's mother was to be protected at all times from any news or information that might disturb her, because of her delicate health. In spite of this delicate condition she lived to be ninety-six.

When Mother returned to California in November 1913, she discovered that the entire ménage—her mother, father, three brothers, grandmother, grandmother's companion, widowed aunt—had left West Oakland and moved into the more congenial foothill community of Piedmont. (Most congenial, of course, because the boy next door was no longer next door.) In this move, which was kept secret from Sylvia, the family discarded many of her treasured possessions, much to her regret. Fortunately for us, however, they did not discard her letters from France.

Albert Salinger Bennett

New York City, 1986

Just a Very Pretty Girl from the Country

[Sylvia Salinger began her trip to France by leaving Oakland and heading in the wrong direction. She went north to Washington State. Harriet had gone on ahead for a rendezvous with a gentleman friend who lived in Seattle, and Sylvia's younger brother Herbert was assigned to escort his sister northward. On September 30, 1912, after completing his assignment and delivering Sylvia into the hands of their aunt, Herbert returned to Oakland. Sylvia later remarked that when Harriet informed her about the rendezvous, she turned purple with rage—the first time Sylvia had witnessed such a phenomenon. It seemed that Harriet's gentleman friend had neglected to tell her that he already had a wife. So the two women finally set off in the right direction, heading eastward across Canada to Toronto and the eastern United States.]

Hotel Knickerbocker, New York City, Oct. 12, 1912

Dear Family:

New York has taken me completely off my feet so I don't know how to write to you—I don't know where to begin. We have just come back from a bus ride along 5th Avenue and Riverside Drive etc. The Drive was all illuminated for the fleet which is now in the river, and it was a wonderful sight! I have never seen so many people in my life. They look like little bits of nothings—there are such quantities of them. And the houses—they look like swell tenements to me. I never heard of people having millions and living in little pent up places like that. Well, we had lunch in the Park, in a lovely little open café. We ate on the porch and it was delightful. Last night we had dinner here, expecting to see all sorts of wonderful things but nothing wonderful happened at all. It is a very lovely (expensive) and very simple place to dine. After dinner we rambled up Broadway a bit—saw all the names I have been hearing all my life and then rambled back and retired early. The lighting effects are something to get excited about—beats even Seattle. One girl jumps rope and a man plays golf and everybody does anything they want him to, up on top of buildings. Speaking of buildings, I shall never recover from the number of just buildings—they go on for miles, all packed in together and all tall and stately looking. I never dreamed there could be so many buildings in the world as I saw today. Well, to get back to yesterday—we had lunch at Child's. It was pretty bad—but we were in a hurry to get to see George Cohan in "Broadway Jones." It was good! We laughed our heads off and when we got home again wondered what we had seen and decided it was a very poor play but most funny.

Yesterday morning was when we arrived. We took a taxi and landed at the Knickerbocker all right but when we started down town for the steamship company—Oh! my, oh! my, we got lost in the subway three different times! I hate, loathe and despise the subway! I wish you could see me talking to one of these giant policemen. You would scream. Harriet always stands on the corner while I go out into the middle of the street to see the policeman. I have great difficulty in making them hear me, because, well, I don't make any attempt to ever see higher than their shoulders. But they are so considerate that I rather like having to talk to them. We managed to get back from downtown and ran to the hotel, took the elevator to the sixth floor and when we got to "609" discovered we were in the wrong hotel! They all look alike! I never in my life laughed so hard as I did when we ran out of that place. It was the Astor and is only across the street!

We phoned to Uncle Frank's friend Mr. Rosenthal tonight and he said he would try to help us with our steamer accomodations. Everything is pretty well filled up, but we have reserved accomodations for Tuesday and Mr. Rosenthal is going to try to get them cheaper for us.

Lots of love,

Sis

[Sylvia was always known as Sister or Sis to her family and intimate friends. To her sister Ruth's children she remained Aunt Sis until her death.]

Hotel Knickerbocker, Oct. 14, 1912

Dear Ruth:

This darned old town has taken me so completely off my feet that I don't seem to be able to come back to earth. We engaged our passage for the Amerika (Holland America line) which sails on Thursday morning and lands us at our destination a week from Friday. Uncle Frank's Mr. Rosenthal told us that was a very fine ship, we have a very fine room and expect to have a very fine trip, etc. Gurden has been lovely! *[Gurden Edwards, a friend of Ruth Salinger Elkus, was then living in New York.]* This morning he escorted us downtown while Harriet procured all the necessaries for sailing Thursday, and then he ran us into a most wonderful aquarium and then left us in the blumin' subway and beat it for the office. Harriet insists upon carrying on an animated conversation with me so I quit. Please write loads: c/o Franco American Bank, 22 Place Vendôme, Paris, France.

Lots of love,

Sis

Hotel Knickerbocker, Oct. 16, 1912

Dearest Ruth:

Aunt Harriet is stealing my bath and I am so sleepy! This morning Gurden went shopping with us and it was great fun. You should have heard his and Harriet's comments on the different hats I tried on—I really felt as if I were somebody when I got through. Nothing was good enough for me. Even the one I got could be improved upon, so they said. Gurden is going to see us off tomorrow and I am glad. It is kind of bum leaving without having some good friend wave you a tender farewell. Harriet is about done, so—

Lots of love,

Sis

An Bord des Dampfers Amerika
den 23 October 1912

Dearest Ruthie:

Harriet is writing home, so why tax my brain and pen with details? It has been—still is—a delightful voyage. The Atlantic is a big ocean. Harriet said yesterday, while we stood gazing over the banister at the clear blue water beneath, that she couldn't realize how very big it is. I said I could perfectly—and then counted the days. We get to Cherbourg Friday noon, according to reports this morning. Hooray! say I, today being Wednesday. We are going home on the Mauretania—I hear it is three hours quicker than the Lusitania. *[The un-armed British passenger liner* Lusitania *was sunk by a German submarine two and one-half years later, on May 7, 1915.]*

But really, to lapse into seriousness it has been wonderful. I am a fine sailor—so they say. Haven't missed a meal and am learning much German. "You teach me German and I will teach you English" get me? Every once in a while the boat goes over on one side so far that we have fears of her never righting herself again.

Gurden saw us off and gave me a beautiful book—French Life in Town and Country by Hannah Lynch. I have read quite a bit of it and it is good reading. However, I don't have much time to read. I am too busy walking—round and round. Then when I get tired of one deck I gaily transfer my affections to the one below. I can truthfully say that I have just about walked from N.Y. to Europe, taking out time of course for meals and sleep. When I walk with an occasional man they beg and implore me not to hurry so—of course there is no hurry but I can't go slow, I am so anxious to get there. Even poor old "Grandpa" was all out of breath last night. I get interested in the conversation and keep speeding up—unconsciously. Grandpa and I discussed the educational situation in America on the first ramble—on the second it was the negro, with Booker T. in the lead. Third—a geographical discussion of California with little me doing all the talking. We meet every evening at half past five and talk till half past six. I wish you could see the performance. Harriet screams. He is about six feet two, extremely "dick" [*stout*] and holds himself perfectly erect, German soldier like. He is over seventy I think and has four grandchildren. His introducing himself was the funniest thing that has happened. Harriet and I were gaily walking the deck when I heard a voice in my ear, "Pardon me, ladies, but can you tell me what raccoon is in German?" Well, the ladies did not know, but further introduction was unnecessary so we are the best of friends. He speaks English fluently. Thank heavens! A little German goes a long way. He has been attending some sort of a council in America and has a brother, a professor at Harvard. He has just completed an essay which he has written on board, and is so sorry that I can't understand German so as to be able to correct it for him. Yesterday he was sick in bed all day and got up at half past five because he knew he must meet me. I love it!

Just had tea! or rather, biscuits—I don't drink tea. [*Tea, coffee, tobacco, alcoholic beverages, and any form of medicine were proscribed for Christian Scientists. Later, however, we shall see Syliva, corrupted by Parisian life, drink quantities of tea and even prepare it for her guests when Marie the maid is out.*] Outside of Grandpa, things are not overly interesting. As Mr. Meyer says, it is the slowest crowd he has ever met on a steamer, and he has crossed many times. Mr. Meyer is the very entertaining, very obliging—father of two and husband of one, who are in London, their home—man at our table. He speaks both Eng. and German so acts as interpreter the greater part of the time. The other two men are the ship's doctor, who said never a word the first two days, but who woke up the first time I went to lunch without Harriet and has stayed awake ever since, and the German youth, aged 36, whose title is Landrat and whom we call the land rat—not to his face, of course. He is the one who is teaching me German. The men all wear evening dress to dinner every night so we do too. Last night was the dance which I did not attend and for which little slight I have been much criticized today. But, I wore my blue silk to dinner and was greeted with much open admiration. It pays to be pretty for foreigners—they love it and let you know they do. I am getting so accustomed to being stared at that I am beginning to think myself almost agreeable looking. Harriet is reciting French verbs in the chair next to me and it is a bit disconcerting.

The boat is full of Herr Doctors just returning from a convention. All big, fat, white-whiskered, and talkative. I just found out who Grandpa is—if you promise not to laugh I shall tell you even though I am in hysterics. Herr Kommerzienrat Otto Munsterberg. Get me? Brother of Hugo. Get me again? *[Hugo Münsterberg, "Grandpa"'s brother, worked with William James at Harvard from 1897 until his death in 1916; he is sometimes referred to as the father of applied psychology.]* You see, while I was waiting for five thirty this evening, I was walking the deck and a man approached and said he had a message for me from Mr. Munsterberg. He had been ill all day and confined to his cabin and was so sorry etc. The funny part was that the man who delivered the message, Herr Kommerzienrat Netter, is a man who has been staring me out of countenance. He sits at the next table. When he approached I almost fainted on the spot and when he told me the whole long story I had hysterics in the middle of it. It's all too much for one so young and charming.

Lots of love,

SIS

[Harriet later wrote a short story, never published, called "An Aunt Is an Aunt." It is set on a liner bound for Europe, and it tells of a beautiful but vapid young girl who enchants all the men on board while her aunt lies seasick in their cabin. When the aunt recovers, it is she to whom the men turn their attentions. Thus Harriet shows how wit and intellect can triumph over mere beauty.]

Hotel Lutetia, Paris, October 28, 1912

Dear Family:

There is a great deal to say, and as usual I don't know where to begin. So much has happened and Paris is such a strange place. But I think I shall begin where I left off in my steamer letter. The last day consisted mostly in packing in the morning and then standing around for hours getting into Cherbourg. During the standing around, Mr. Netter came up to me and told me that Grandpa was very sick and would not be able to say good bye, which of course was most sad. Well, during this time Mr. Netter told me of a hotel in Berlin and said it was new, and he should like so much to have me stop there because it was in his neighborhood and he could call, also he has two motor cars, etc. Well, about a half hour before we landed who should come sauntering up but Grandpa. He could not stand it—had to see me before I left to tell me what a lovely girl I am—vast intellect, so entertaining etc. It was a pity that I had given up my piano but surely he had some influence and knew I would take it up again. Then he went back to bed. Ain't it funny!

The going on board the tender (the little ship that landed us) and waving good-bye to the people on the Amerika was a beautiful sight. It was all so jolly and gay, only about forty of us disembarked for Cherbourg, while the whole ship, even the steerage, was out to wave to us. It was lovely! And when we got a little way off and could see our Amerika it looked so big it scared me.

Well, at Cherbourg the suitcases had to go through customs. Harriet went ahead to get window seats in the compartment while I stayed behind to be customed. The man threw a hundred questions at me—French—and everything I said "no" to. It went off all right, however. Then, when I tried to get through the gate, after waiting about half an hour for Harriet to come back, I couldn't pass without a ticket, and I couldn't tell the man anything. Finally, I got desperate and ran past him and out to the train. Then while I was sitting comfortably in the train, Harriet having gone for a telegraph office to wire Mike—*[Harriet telegraphed Michael Stein the time of the boat train so he could meet them—standard practice for Americans en route to Paris.]* I saw my suitcases disappearing in the distance and had to chase them. It was most exciting! After six hours on the train we landed in Paris and—Sara and Mike and Allen and Gertrude and Alice were there to meet us. It was a joyous meeting, Sarah declaring that she was gladder to see me than to see Harriet. After going through customs with the trunks, Alice and Gertrude got into one cab and disappeared—our trunks got into another and the rest of us in still another. Then the two cabs had a race up to this hotel. We are only here for a few days waiting for a pension to be emptied. We have engaged two rooms there. The Steins stayed here awhile Friday evening and then we went to sleep in wonderful beds. I have had absolutely no motion of the steamer and I think that is rather unusual. Nicht wahr? Which reminds me I must drop German and take up French.

Saturday morning we woke up at ten thirty and had breakfast in bed. Mike called for us at one and we went to Sara's. The first impression of Sarah's was a never to be forgotten one. *[The Steins' home in a converted church on the rue Madame (see plate 9) housed their extensive display of post-impressionist art. (Sarah Stein herself had studied painting for a time in the studio of Henri Matisse.) On Saturday nights Sarah and Gertrude held rival salons at which each showed off her latest acquisitions.]* I could not make it out, but finally decided the thing to do was to concentrate on one picture until I could see something—well, I have hopes for myself—in several of them I could see what was meant—I mean the object—but in few could I see beauty. In fact, there were three in which I could see beauty—and from what I hear that is doing rather well. And I did it all by myself, too. Sarah is so wonderful that any place she was in would seem homelike so that side of the question begins and ends right there. Well, the next move was to go pension hunting. We climbed stairs and went into the most peculiar looking rooms I have ever seen. We finally took rooms at the first one we went into. We also called on Sallie and Laurie Strauss and they are the sweetest couple and have the cunningest place—it is all just about the size of our living room—but is really very home-like. I expect to see a great deal of them. This morning, Sunday, we went to Church.

Then we went to Sarah's to lunch and it was quite a relief after the blumin' a la carte eating of months. After lunch Allen took me to see Paris. We did not walk—we ran—just everywhere and through everything—Allen giving me the historical significance to every piece of everything as we ran by. His chief object was not to have me see anything deffinitely, but just to kind of get an impression, so that I should fall in love with Paris immediately. It was a funny afternoon! I ran through the Luxembourg Gardens, through the Luxembourg Gallery—just imagine it, you who have seen it—through the Clunie Museum—through some funny little church—through Notre Dame—and along the river—it was not to see anything, remember, but just to get an idea of the possibilities of Paris. He certainly is some youth. I forgot the Pantheon. Then he rushed me to Gertrude's and he vanished. *[Allan Stein, then seventeen years old and seven years her junior, was instantly smitten with Sylvia. After her return to America, he continued to ply her with passionate, charming, and imaginative love letters, which she treasured for many years.]* I was at Gertrude's about two minutes when Harriet came, and we had tea. Gertrude is the biggest, most awfully dressed person I have ever seen. Of course after all the stories, I expected to see something quite out of the ordinary—but, after having been with her for five hours and not taking my eyes off her face one minute, I shall be almost as surprised the next time I see her, I am sure. We also stayed there to supper—which Alice prepared, the maid being out, and which was most good. Sad to say, I am beginning to notice food, I have so much of it, it seems.

After supper we sat around and talked, Leo flitting in and out as if we weren't there at all, after the first greeting and introduction. Then Gertrude and Alice walked us home and Harriet almost had heart failure when she thought Gertrude might come up with us.

Will you please keep my letters. I should like to have them when I come back, instead of keeping a diary.

Lots of love,

Sis

Hotel Lutetia, Oct. 29, 1912

Dear Family:

I called on Laurie Strauss yesterday and displayed my voice—I was most agreeably surprised! He is going to give me lessons—says I have a very sweet little voice! that I can very easily be taught to carry a tune, etc. I am to have a latch key and just run in and practice whenever I want. Isn't it lovely? I can't practice at the pension but I think it will be even better practicing at Sally's. Laurie Strauss, by the way, has been doing big things. His teacher has given him permission to use his name in teaching, and that, over here with a big man, is a sure sign. He is getting one engagement after the other and his voice is beautiful. So, by studying with him I am incidentally getting the method of one of the biggest men here now. I would tell you his name, but can't think of it just this minute. *[It was the renowned tenor Jean de Reszke, later spelled by Harriet as "De Retzke," who had retired to Paris in 1902 to teach.]*

Yesterday morning Harriet, Mike, and I went shopping at the Bon Marche. It was very interesting (we each bought a pair of gloves). But, you know, it looks just like Salingers except, of course, it is so much larger—3 big buildings all used for one store. Then we went to a funny little place—Harriet and I—and had a most wonderfully simple lunch and what do you think? You take a plate and spoon and go to the shelves and select your own little tart for dessert! Harriet had to bring mine, I couldn't do the work for the first time, but promised to the second.

In the afternoon we went to the very nice Strauss' to tea. Mike and Sarah were there—also a Mr. Poorman—a successful painter who only talks French and German—no English! so the conversation was most difficult. Well, they all left and I stayed on for my interview of which I have already written. Then Mr. Strauss took me to Steins, where Harriet and I had been invited to supper. Those meals are wonderful! We never eat here any more except for breakfast. After supper, Harriet and Sarah and Mike had much conversation while Allan entertained me in the other room. Allen flew upstairs and brought down a little bashful sixteen year-old friend who is studying English in school. It was a lot of fun—each trying to make the other understand something and Allen in the middle acting as interpreter. We got home late! This morning I called on Sarah and Harriet stayed home. We went to lunch today at the same funny little place, but did not eat any tarts, instead, selected a vegetable sandwich. Tonight we go to Gertrude's to supper.

I'll leave this open and write more tomorrow. *[Sylvia, however, finds it necessary to skip a day.]*

Yesterday was such a busy day that I had no time to write at all, but I shall begin where I left off. I must tell you of the funny little letter box we have in our room. We may be sitting perfectly quiet when all of a sudden—pop! down comes a letter into the little box—it has a glass front, so sometimes we can even see who it is from. You ought to see Harriet and me when we come into the room after having been out for awhile—each one takes a little peek at the letter box. Well, now, to continue— we went to Gertrude's to supper. She had on a big loose black corduroy robe and looked quite extraordinary! In fact, if she did not dress like such a freak on the street she would be really handsome! We enjoyed supper so much and then sat in the salon and talked till almost twelve. We saw Leo's room this time, too. It is very beautiful—but of course I can't begin to describe it. He has a table he designed himself—and I did so want it for the living room! Leo lives alone, mostly in this room—he does not eat with Gertrude and Alice at all. He and Harriet had a very nice time for a while but I couldn't do the work so I rambled in to talk to Gertrude and Alice. Alice has such faith in me—it is strange— you know, she always did think I was something and the funny part of it is, she still does. *[When Sylvia was in her eighties, she was confronted with the proliferation of publicity about the lesbian relationship between Gertrude and Alice. "Oh!" she said. "That's probably why they tried to keep beautiful me away from that household." Indeed, the appearances of Gertrude and Alice in Sylvia's letters will gradually diminish.]*

Yesterday morning I took my first lesson! I love it! The most encouragement I got was when Mr. Strauss turned around and said, "Hasn't anyone ever told you you had a sweet voice?" Kind of nice, huh? I answered by telling him I never had a chance because it hurt everybody's ears when they heard me. He is going to practice with me the first few times to start me off right.

Also, I have a French teacher, I think. She lives right across from our pension, into which we move Tuesday, by the way—and if she has time, she shall be my lady. Speaking of French—I was alone in the room today and someone knocked and much to my surprise I found myself saying "Qui est la?" When the volley of French came back I realized what I had done, but decided to stay with it, so I said "Entrez" which the chamber-maid did. She asked me if her helper could come, too, so I said he could and then there followed a few questions and answers and I am quite proud of myself.

Yesterday Harriet and Mrs. Stein and I went to Mrs. Morrison's to lunch. We had a lovely lunch, very prettily served, and then sat around and talked all afternoon. Mrs. Morrison is American—the wife of an English painter who has had some success in England. Most of the afternoon was spent in Sarah's and Harriet's trying to explain Jewish family life to our hostess. It was funny! I don't think the poor woman understands yet just exactly what really is the point of it. All she could say was, "Then it has its disadvantages, also." Mrs. Morrison lives on the other side of the river and we walked home along the river while it was growing dark. It is very beautiful! It gets dark between half past four and five and I can't get used to it. We went to Stein's to supper and enjoyed it all over again. I am still on the same picture at the Steins and when I see some beauty in it shall pass on to the next—but so far, I haven't advanced very much. I can see a little, to be sure, but that isn't enough. After supper we went to Church.

This morning Alice's dressmaker came into fix my blue dress, which has lately sprung a tail in the back. She ripped the entire hem, measured it and sewed it up by hand, sewing the tape on and all, in practically no time at all. I have never seen anything like it—I don't think I could have done it in half the time with a machine. And it is perfectly done.

The bread and butter is the most wonderful I have ever tasted, or dreamed of tasting. You know how I loved French bread at home, well, when I see the people walking down the street with these loaves as big as a house I want to bite right into them. I would love to bring a few home instead of gloves, but I am afraid it would be just a little impractical. Something I want to tell you about that will interest you, Papa. This hotel is built and run just like an American hotel—all the luxuries, even the high prices, café a la carte and one table d'hote and everything a high class American hotel would have—and it has been put up and run by the Bon Marche, which is just across the square. What think you of that for an example of a business head? I am trying to think of some more so as to get my money's worth out of the stamp, but the chamber-maid just came in again to open the beds, and threw such a volley of French at me all over again that everything has gone right out of my head. I am such a fool—instead of saying I don't understand

I make a try at it and keep getting in wrong all the time. They say that it is the best way to learn the language so I shall continue to get in wrong.

Lots of love,

Sis.

Dear Family:

I want to write beginning where I left off last time, but how can I when I don't know where I did that little thing? I have a hunch that it was Thursday, so here goes from there. The mornings are mostly taken up with sleeping *[Harriet interlines: "and consuming endless rolls & marmalade."]* and then going to Strauss' to practice, so that is not too exciting to write. We have an inside room here and the light that comes in is so dark that we just sleep on. *[Harriet crosses out "we" and substitutes "I" and adds "and Harriet waits for me to wake up."]* Laurie has been practicing with me right along, which of course makes it just like a lesson each day, but that little stunt will be discontinued shortly as he does not seem to think it is the best plan. Friday afternoon we went to tea at Mrs. de Buyko's. There were quite a number of people there, among them being a Mr. and Mrs. Maybe. Isn't that an awful thing? It was a frightful bore *[Harriet: "Except for the food which was plentiful."]* and I was glad when Sarah said she had to leave and would take us home to supper with her. The maid was out so Sarah and Allen got supper. It was just like a Sunday night at

17

home. Sarah scrambled the eggs for the chosen few and Allen fixed a most beautiful pancake for him and me. We came home late, as usual, and I steered Harriet home just as if I had been living in this little quarter all my life and she had been visiting for a week. *[Harriet: "Such a wichtig macher (big deal)! From Oakland she comes."]*

Saturday night we went to dinner at a very nice café just next door and enjoyed it muchly. I ate some oysters that are considered superb and I considered them superbly rotten, but they were expensive so I had to eat them. They had a rather peculiar metally taste that makes one want to baa-baa while consuming same. *[Harriet: "She's mixing sheep & goats—goats eat cans but they don't baa-baa." This, by the way, is the only time Harriet edits a letter of Sylvia's.]*

After dinner we went to Sarah's for a Saturday night. There were a number of Americans there. Everybody just walked in and looked at pictures and walked out again—except Sarah's friends, who stayed. Tomorrow afternoon Alice and Gertrude are going downtown with us. I don't think we shall purchase much, but expect to see a great deal. The French babies are the most beautiful I have ever seen. I don't think I have seen one plain looking baby since I arrived. Saturday I am going to Miss Aldrich, a friend of Harriet's. *[Mildred Aldrich, who was in her sixties when Sylvia met her, had lived in Paris for many years. She earned her living buying French-language plays for American theatrical producers. Her book,* A Hilltop on the Marne, *published by Houghton Mifflin in 1915, described the famous World War I battle that took place virtually in her front garden.]*

Lots of love to you all,

Sis.

Dear Family:

Hooray for Wilson! [*Woodrow Wilson was elected the twenty-eighth president of the United States on November 5, 1912.*]

We are moved—we moved yesterday morning and when we came into our rooms we were delighted! The open fireplace was ablaze—the little bed looked so inviting and there was a big plant of chrysanthemums in each room—which Alice had so thoughtfully sent. I worked unpacking the various trunks and trying to put things away in the funny little closets—that accomplished, the bell rang for lunch and we went down—to the minute, as all proper pensioners do. The table was a surprise—I think there are more than twenty-five people—and, well, it was too much—three were French. You can't get away from Americans, and I don't want to. The subject of politics was discussed at great length, yesterday having been the day at the polls. They live on discussions here instead of food, but that's coming later. After lunch I wondered what there was inside of me that had spoken up and said "Non, merci" when I really did want a second helping. After lunch I hied me to practice. After said practice lesson, I returned to find Mike and Harriet comfortably settled, talking away to beat the band. It was raining yesterday so it got dark at about three—so, as we have not enough lighting facilities yet, we decided to take a walk. We went to Gertrude's to thank Alice and then we went to interview my French teacher. She lives on the fourth floor of a place just about a block away. After the interview, when we were coming down, I stopped at the third—petrified. There were three perfectly good American college fellows—talking perfectly good American college talk, and I couldn't move. I wanted to give 'em the Oski, but I didn't. *[University of California athletes were urged on to greater glory with a battle cry containing the phrase "Oski Wow-wow!"]* Anyhow, I go for my first lesson this afternoon.

Dinner was at seven, and just to show that I can dress for dinner, I changed from one blue dress to another and wore my watch on the outside. I did not refuse a second helping! After dinner, Harriet and I came upstairs and she said, "Somehow I don't feel finished"—and dove into an orange. I said in plain words, "I am starved"—also diving into an orange. Then we ate some candy and finally I suggested "Why not go house-keeping?" It was done! We put on our hats and coats and ran around to the Steins. They were a bit startled, but when we were all settled down once more they were glad. So, at the present moment, Harriet and Mike are out looking for a furnished apartment. At Steins I ate some apple fritters that were left over from dinner—then we had tea and innumerable cookies. There was no doubt but what I was hungry.

This morning I had a singing lesson and loved it more than ever.

Lunch is over! and I feel more comfortable having discovered that lunch is dinner—and dinner really quite satisfying. Harriet came back having found nothing—but she went to very few places. Anyhow, we have to give our lady here at least one week's notice, so, what's the hurry? Harriet just went to lie down and she said "I'll see you tonight" meaning three o'clock. The house-keeping idea is more than mere food, you understand. It means that we can be alone at table—very desirable—that we can have as many people in as often as we want, to tea or lunch or any time. And, from what I hear, there will probably be a great deal of that as there are so many American people here. There is a regular crowd of girls just about my age, and Sally says there is no end to them. I rather like the way they do the social stunt. You don't go anywhere to spend the afternoon at all—you go at half past four or even five, to tea, and then stay till about six or half past. Everyone suppers at seven. I am going to my French lesson now so—Did I tell you I am taking a lesson every day—just for a while to get a good start—every day but Thursday and Sunday. Thursday has been taken out because Allen has no school on that day and I shall probably ride and Sunday is the day of rest. There is no swimming at all in "our set," so that hope has died a natural death. *[Sylvia recommences her letter on the following day.]*

Nov. 7

We are still here—after having run around town quite a bit, unsuccessfully. Apartment hunting is not quite as simple as it sounds. We want, first to be near the Steins—then we want a bath, and so few on this side have them. We are probably too particular, but still have hopes. The dinner conversation this evening was terribly funny. We were speaking of how hard it is to fold the napkins— they are so large. So, someone said they never unfolded theirs at all, except, of course, once a week to turn it over. The conversation then passed on to sheets—they are changed every fifteen days—towels, two, changed once a week. They did not say how often the tablecloth changes, but I'd hate to guess. I have had two French lessons—and, really, I enjoy them. Outside of the woman's wanting to

teach me the whole French language each time I go,
I think she will be very good. Another good thing
about housekeeping will be that I can have a piano,
which may be rented very cheap. *[The rest of the November 6–7 letter is missing.]*

November 9, 1912

Dear Family:

Yesterday afternoon Alice and Gertrude went
downtown shopping with us. We went in an auto-
taxi. The chauffeurs drive like mad and it is as much
as your life is worth to get in a mix-up in a crowded
street. They say that the law here is—the fellow
who gets run over is in the wrong and is conse-
quently sued for stopping traffic. I don't believe it,
however. Well, Harriet took her fur coat down to
have remodelled and it is sure to be quite beautiful.
I purchased a set of white fox, which is lovely! I get
excited when I even think about it—they are being
made up. Alice looks at me so pityingly that I feel
as if I had committed a great sin by dressing the
way I do. She thinks everything I have—which
really is practically nothing—most awful and I can
see she is itching to get her hands on me. I am
going to let her dress me from head to foot, and
then I shall have Mike take some snaps of me and
send them home.

After purchasing the furs we went to tea at one
of the fashionable places. It is very interesting just
to sit and watch the French men and women walk
in and out—it is muchly like a parade—the women
are so perfectly put together. Then we walked
around on the Rue something or other and around

the Place Vendome, which was all lit up, it having gotten dark by then, and which was most beautiful! I saw, for the first time, some of the much talked about French cars—they are wonders! Then we auto-bussed again—home. Isn't it funny that people don't look at Gertrude and Alice? I thought surely that we would be the center of attraction everywhere but not at all—they don't attract one half the attention that ladies of fashion do.

This morning I spent the greater part of the time running around in my kimono waiting to get a bath. I finally did manage to get one and since they cost 1 franc I hate to get out when I do get in. But— Then to Laurie's to practice, after which Laurie ran around with me hunting apartments. Then home to lunch. Harriet didn't show up for lunch at all, and let me tell you some of the funny things that happened. I don't remember how we got there but I found myself in the middle of a discussion of the American negro. I—against eight Southerners. Can you picture it? I said something about not having any feeling on the subject at all—they weren't any different from anyone else particularly etc. etc. Well, one lady (?) said that was the first time she had ever heard a decent white talk like that. I assured her I considered myself quite decent. Another asked me if I would marry a negro—and I said that one does not marry anyone that one happens to hold on the same footing. Well, it went on and I finally laughed it off and lunch was over. After lunch I met a little lady in the hall, and she stopped me and said she had to tell me how wonderfully I carried off that very unpleasant conversation. She said that she—and she looks like such a gentle lady—always got mad—she said she was just boiling inside and praised me up to the ceiling for being so decent. After that I came into my room and there came a knock at the door and another lady entered. She said she wanted to know my name etc. and I wondered what in the world was coming. She took the liberty to come to my room because she had to tell me how remarkably I had conducted myself during the most awful slanderous conversation she had ever been witness to. She said she never would have stood for being spoken to in such an unseemly manner and wished to congratulate me on my gracious manner etc.—said she had never seen anything to equal it in a woman of the world—not alone in a young girl. Then she was gone. Well, I am yet to recover! (I forgot to say she is from Chicago and she only wished I were from Chicago—the highest compliment she could pay me.)

After all the excitement I went to find Harriet. She was at the Steins and had had lunch there. She had secured an apartment and was making arrangements. It is only about two blocks from the Steins.

Back again—I have been to tea at Mildred's— it was a good thing it was dark. I never got such a shock in my life! "Mildred" is an old lady in a lavender dressing gown! Mike & Sarah were there also. On the way home from "Mildred"'s I had the good fortune of seeing a French chemical engine just getting ready to go home from a false alarm. I am glad I saw it—I shall be very careful not to set fire to anything. The men are beautiful! How they must hate to get mussed up. When they drove off sitting up there with their arms folded, looking so handsome, I couldn't believe that they were firemen at all. They looked much more like a passing show. *[Sylvia's letter begins again after a day's hiatus.]*

The most awful thing has happened to me—I can't find out who won the Big Game! *[The annual game between the football teams of the University of California and Stanford University—the Big Game—was always an important event in the lives of the Salinger children.]* If somebody don't write it, I'll cable sure. I was tickled to death that Oakland won the pennant. *[The Oakland Oaks played baseball in the Pacific Coast League.]* Yesterday morning we went to church—that is, Harriet went to the French service, while I went to practice, then I went to the English service with Sallie. After said service we, Harriet and I, went to a café to dinner. It was wonderful! We had butter on our bread, we had potatos with our meat. It was almost too good to be true. After dinner Harriet came home and I went to Gertrude's. I stayed there for quite a while talking to Alice about Clarence. I made as much of a contribution as I could, not having seen him for some time. *[Alice Toklas's brother Clarence was one of Sylvia's many rejected suitors. He committed suicide more than a decade later; to the end of her life Sylvia thought it was because of her rejection of him.]* Then Harriet woke up and we walked around to Sarah's, stayed there for a little while and came back to supper.

Last night Harriet went to bed and Allen and I went to the Norledges. Mr. & Mrs. Stein were there, too. They talked art and I learned so much I don't know where to put it. It was fine—I just sat and listened—never opened my mouth the whole evening and loved it. When I went to Laurie's this morning to practice he was heating water for a bath and you should have seen it. As he said, he had fried water, boiled water, baked water and casseroled water.

They have to heat it to carry it into the tub. The stove looked so funny.

This afternoon Harriet and I went shopping. I bought a dress—velvet old rose color, I think. It is so pretty I adore myself in it. I wish you could see Harriet cross a crowded street. It is an awful thing. She starts and then runs back again and says, "I just can't do it." I suggested taking a cab across, and I think I will have to one of these days. We move Thursday—have taken the apartment for two months and are now waiting for a maid. If we like it, as we no doubt shall, of course we can keep it. Our front windows face Steins back windows so I expect to arrange some kind of a signal system. Mr. Stein just came in with some home made cookies. *[The letter continues again after another hiatus.]*

Nov. 14

Sunday morning we went to Church and after Service we went home with Sarah to dinner. Mr. & Mrs. Norledge, the temporary readers, also were there. *[The services in Christian Science churches are conducted by two Readers—one reading selections from the Bible, the other reading explanatory passages from* Science and Health *by Mary Baker Eddy.]* Mike doesn't allow any serious conversation at the table so it was most pleasant. After dinner Sarah and Harriet and I went to the Grand Salon. It is beautiful! They are having the Autumn showing just now. The main attraction is Matisse. He has two things that are supposed to be tres wonderful! I can see the coloring wonder of it, but as far as grace, etc. are concerned, I don't get it at all. Still, I am not supposed to, they tell me. One interesting thing about the Salon is the display of wall papers that have been designed just as all the other arts are worked out. Some of them are very lovely. Then, another thing is the rooms—bedrooms—drawing rooms—tea rooms—dining rooms—libraries—everything complete—each little room a thing apart from everything else. There was one, a child's bedroom, that was the prettiest I have ever seen. They are completely furnished, even to the books on the shelves. It is a splendid way to get ideas. After the Salon we went back to Sarah's to rest. We walked along the river for a little way and when we crossed one of the bridges there were hundreds of people standing there watching the sunset! It was glorious! The Steins went to dinner with us at the nice café next door and we had a very pleasant evening. You know, when you finish eating you just kind of sit around and enjoy yourself. The people at the next table were playing cards.

We move in the morning.

Lots of love,

Sis

31 Rue de Vaugirard, November 16, 1912

Dearest Ruthie:

We are settled! Thank heavens! Our apartment is very pleasant and home-like and we are comfortable. We have a kitchen, two bedrooms, dining-room and salon, or as we call it home, a living-room. We have a maid, who is pretty and young and most competent! She thinks I am plumb crazy because I am constantly running into the kitchen to ask for things and forgetting the word as soon as she looks at me. And I can't get enough to eat!

I am really working! I haven't time for anything at all. I take a French lesson every day and it is a terrible thing when your teacher thinks you are intellectual. She gives me just about three times as much work as any ordinary mortal could possibly digest. She apologized yesterday for stacking it on by saying what a fine mind I have etc. She said it in English, too! so I didn't misunderstand. Harriet says she must have a great many dull pupils. I am taking two lessons a week now in singing, as I have a piano (rented at $2.00 per mo.) and can accomplish so much more. Laurie has taken such an interest in my little voice that I almost feel as though I ought to spend most of my time there.

Harriet has gone out for a walk and I am here in fear and trembling—I know the cleaner is coming and I can't talk to her. It seems so funny, all these people look so kind of human and still they can't understand me. Do you realize that I don't even know who won the Big Game and it is a whole week off already. That is almost more than I can stand. Mail day isn't 'till Tuesday.

Lots of love,

Sis.

November 21, 1912

Dear Family:

It is ten o'clock and I have just finished two big fat hours of studying French! Today was a most complete, nice day. I worked all morning, chiefly practicing. After lunch Allen & I took a horse-bus, one of the few left in the city, and rode way up on top—to the Louvre. Riding thro town that way was very pleasant indeed and at the Louvre I got the surprise of my life. I didn't know it was so big and beautiful from the outside. Then, when we went in, and the winged victory greeted us as we came up the lovely stairs, it was a nice feeling through and through. I found myself running around looking for familiar things and I found quite enough to satisfy me. Now that I know where it is and how to get there, it will be rather difficult staying away. It is a marvelous place! From there I went with Harriet to tea at Madame Humbert's. She lives in a very swell apartment on the other side and has a daughter eighteen who is so beautiful I just sat and gazed at her. We went up in one of those funny little elevators—to the sixth floor. We came home in the underground, which first becomes an elevated and crosses the river, and then plunges down into a subway again. Crossing the river, with all the lights ablaze and the Eifel tower in the distance, was a most wonderful sight. *[The letter is continued the next day.]*

Nov. 22

Wednesday I took a lesson in the morning and a French lesson in the afternoon. Then, wonder of wonders, I summed up enough courage to go to the Bon Marche to buy some wool and a crochet needle—to make a shawl for Sallie's Baby. I got along beautifully! even got the right change, and was so fussed up about it that it took the rest of the day to come back to earth. Wednesday night Mrs. Morrison, whose husband is out of town, came in to dinner, and we went to church together. Harriet reads Science and Health in German, thinks it in English, and hears it read in French. Gee! I wish I could! I have a very hard time trying to use the little French I know. Yesterday the maid asked me if she should polish my riding boots. I was more than willing to have them polished, but was afraid she might use the black instead of tan and, I couldn't tell her. Allen happened in at the crucial moment and when he explained it to her, she went into hysterics. She thinks I am one big joke. Tonight Harriet's friend Mildred is coming in to dinner—This afternoon we are going to the Hydes for tea—Mrs. Hyde and her three daughters are all very nice and very good Scientists. Tomorrow night we are going to Gertrude's to dinner and shall stay for the evening to see the people who come to look at the pictures and discuss art. I am trying to think of everything all at once so that I can get this off for the steamer mail.

Just read this over and discovered that I hadn't told you about my most wonderful fox set! I adore it! Last night we ran around to Steins for a few minutes and they screamed! I had to wear the foxes even though I had on my old coat under them. They are so big and fluffy and soft and white and beautiful!

Lots of love,

Sis

[The following letter is written by Harriet to her mother. Grandma Levy, then eighty-six, had never learned to read English, so Mrs. Peabody, her companion, had to read the letter to her.]

Dear Mama:

You wouldn't believe that any city could be so
dark so early in the afternoon. It is 4:30—as I
write—and everywhere the lights are lit. Some days
it is dark at 3:30. They say that the weather is getting to be like London where the fogs are low and
make the city very dark.

Paris has changed very much since I was here.
Everywhere there are new buildings going up, big
apartment houses. A big avenue has been cut
through and here on both sides are big buildings,
very modern. And the streets are crowded with
machines.

I think the beginning of the new order of
things has begun, for people are no longer satisfied
with the old apartments without baths and lights.
On the steamer we met a German professor who
told me that America had set the fashion in Europe
of hotel rooms with baths. He said that he wasn't
surprised that they had baths with every room in
New York—because the city was so dirty, that they
needed them. We are so comfortable in this little
place, that we took for two months. We couldn't
stand the food at the pension. There was all meat
and no vegetables—and no butter. Sylvia would
leave the table hungry every meal. Here we have
what we want and it is so much pleasanter.

For lunch today we had hard boiled eggs—
halved—with a tomato sauce. It was so good. The
tomatoes were cooked slowly with onion & pars-
ley—and when quite smooth—strained I suppose,
poured over the eggs. It makes a fine lunch dish.
The other night we had a squab surrounded by

chestnuts—cooked like squash or puree of pota-
toes. That was good too. And for dessert one night
we had a round little pudding of rice with cooked
half pears standing all around. That was good too.

Then we have an omellete filled with little
pieces of bread that have been toasted in butter
first.

But it's so funny how they serve here. There
are no big joints as we have them. A roast beef is
a most unimportant little affair, very well done—
never rare. The meat is served by itself—Then po-
tatoes as a separate course: then a salad—& then
dessert. The salad is for the most part—just lettuce
with fine herbs. The other day we had a guinea hen.
It looked as big as a turkey with all the black and
white feathers—but when it is stripped, it is hardly
bigger than a chicken. It tastes like a chicken with
just a flavor of game.

They eat tame & wild rabbit here a good deal—
and also venison—which you can buy by the slice.
I wanted some wine for myself—so I went to a
large wine shop across the street—one of the
branches of a big establishment. Well you should
have seen the attention I received—as I did not
know what I wanted—the man opened many bottles
for me and poured wine into many glasses. It frightened me, because they said that I could not tell unless I drank about a half a glass of each. I finally
selected one at 20 cts. a bottle, which I think very
good. And I bought little samples of curacao and
kirsh that they put up in tiny sample bottles at 10
cts. a bottle.

We have not been to a theatre yet. I think that,
as Sylvia does not understand French, that I shall
go to the matinees alone. Sarah Bernhardt leaves
for her American tour—so I shall not see her. And I

see that Isadora Duncan has signed for an American tour in Spring. She is building a theatre here in which to introduce Greek dancing. We have tickets for a concert on Sunday—the Lamoureux concert, which are the second best concerts in the world. It seems that the Boston Symphonie ranks first. This afternoon I am going to the Louvre to see some pictures and then to tea to some Americans who have lived here four years. On Saturday nights we generally go to Sarah's. Last Saturday there were about 45 people there of whom 22 stayed to tea.

I think that Sylvia is going to have a very good voice. It grows bigger all the time. I want one too.

I get on with French much better than when I was here. The rest seems to have done me good.

That's all for to-day. Give my love to Mrs. Peabody.

Your loving

HARRIET

November 25

Dear Family:

Last night we went over to Steins for a while and Allen and his friend Felix entertained me by trying to teach me French and by giving a little boxing exhibition. Yesterday afternoon we went to the Lamoureux concert. Here is the programme: Symphonie (Beethoven), La Chasse du Prince Arthur (Guy Raparty), Symphonie (Caesar Franck) and two more things which were substitutes for Alice Dumas who was to sing and was sick. Also, in the middle, a Liszt Concerto played with orchestral ac-

33

companiment by Joseph Lhevinne. What do you think of that for an afternoon's performance? After the first two numbers Harriet said she was going to buy tickets for next Sunday immediately! After the first four, she went to sleep and by the time we got out we were both just about all in. We are going next Sunday but have promised ourselves to leave before the end. Bauer is going to play. *[It is interesting to note how Sylvia records the famous names of the period. The English pianist Harold Bauer, for example, is never given a first name. Nor are violinists Jan Kubelik and Fritz Kreisler ("Kreissler" in Sylvia's orthography), singer Nellie Melba, dancers Anna Pavlova and Mikhail Mordkin, or of course Henri Matisse. On the other hand, it is Sarah Bernhardt, Isadora Duncan, and Lilli Lehmann—in full.]* The theatre is beautiful—all lovely comfortable chairs all alike everywhere except some have arms and some haven't. The women were so beautifully dressed—every kind of fur imaginable and they wear them so picturesquely. And when we first sat down I kept looking around and wondering what was so distinctly strange about the audience. Nobody takes their hats off—men or women. And another thing, more than half the place were men—something you never see home. After the first number the men's hats came off, but the women all sat as if they expected to stay about ten minutes.

Saturday afternoon we went downtown and I ordered a coat—couldn't get one ready made—it is to be of black stuff, sort of plush, looks like the fur Harriet's coat is made of. I shall wear my white fox with it and expect to look most handsome. When Harriet tried to tell the cab man to take us to the tea room at the Place Vendome she kept saying over and over again "Le tea room" and the poor man looked so dazed till I suddenly realized what she was saying and came to the rescue. The tea-room is a funny little place—everybody successful comes there. They can be successful in any way at all—then they go to the Tea Room—any way at all means—in art, in finance, socially, or even successful bums of both sexes. One woman was perfectly perfect—a sable coat that covered her all up—diamonds and pearls the size you read about and her face as well done as anything you ever could see. Then another woman came in in the stiffest tailor suit, with the stiffest hat and the stiffest little bouquet stuck in her button-hole. There were many men—all kinds—even my very nice-looking man at the bank came in with the dizziest blonde ever. I guess that's why we never get any mail—he's too busy to forward it.

Saturday night we went to Gertrude's to dinner—Gertrude has a good cook. After dinner we sat in the salon and the funny people came to look at pictures and get Gertrude's opinion on any subject in the world. Alice was talking to a funny young man from Mexico, who is a composer—what kind I don't know. She finally managed to bring me into the conversation. I had been reading in the corner. We got along beautifully discussing babies. You know, these artist people are the limit to try to hold an everyday conversation with. It's the hardest work ever! They just sit all kind of sprawled out and let you do the talking. If you get tired and stop—there is dead silence until you begin again. It is most nerve-racking, to say the least. Gertrude makes a beautiful hostess—she wears a big black corduroy robe, very loose and flowing, and really looks quite imposing. When she is dressed like that and in her own studio she looks very handsome. She talks to everybody about everything. I never saw anyone who knows so much, except of course Sarah and Mike (don't worry, I'm not that intimate to their faces).

I got a letter last night telling me all about the game! Such a relief—I have been wondering who won the blumin' thing. I just stopped for a few minutes to practice a bit and find it most difficult playing the air and the accompaniment and singing in French—It seems to me that talking in French is enough work without trying to sing the blumin' language. Harriet says if you put some little round onions in with the carrots when you cook them, they are tres delicious—also serve them avec onions.

Lots of love,

Sis

November 29, 1912

Dear Family:

Life has been rather strenuous since my last letter. Harriet is writing about our Thanksgiving dinner, so I won't. It was a great success. Yesterday afternoon I went riding with Allen out in the country. It was a beautiful day and we had a glorious ride! There were two aeroplanes—monos—flying up over us the whole time, which helped to make things exciting. They are not allowed to fly over Paris proper. Last night when I went to my room, I found a big box of all kinds of assorted milk chocolates, with a verse to Sylvia, and a little book with a French story started therein—what the story means

I have yet to know, but the verse I could translate a little of. It was very well done, and so well put up. Allen, of course.

Wednesday night Harriet and I went shopping. I fitted my coat, which is an beauty. I hate to wear it over here where you can't see it. And I bought a hat—cutest thing ever! It has a rose top, with a little seal-skin around next to the face, and then a feather (more like a quill) very thin and long, that goes straight up in the front like a question mark. The hat is about the size of a peanut. When the man brought the hat I wanted to find out whether it would go with my dress, which is on the rose also, so I took the man with the hat and started around to Stein's. When I got halfway there, I discovered I had forgotten the dress and in quite fluent French I managed to tell him I had forgotten something and for him to <u>listen</u> instead of <u>wait</u>, but he finally understood and then we were all right. Sarah approved of the hat color etc. so all is well. If my coat comes, I shall probably wear said new costume to Steins on Saturday night. Tonight Gertrude and Alice are coming in to dinner. Tomorrow night we go to Steins and Sunday night Laurie and Sallie are coming in to supper—the maid goes out. Allen gave me the Examiner account of the big game, so I expect to know more about it this time than I ever did before.

Lots of love,

Sis

Dear Family:

Gertrude and Alice were in to dinner Friday night. Outside of the stove being out of order, and the weather being exceedingly chilly it was a most successful evening.

Saturday night Harriet stayed home and I went over to Steins. There were very few people there, and nobody came to look at the pictures at all. Sometimes there are such mobs and other times there are so very few. Sallie and Laurie and another man—that's all. Mr. Stein played the Victrola until we were mis & mas for the blumin' thing. We had tea and that accompanied by the vic. Sallie and I looked at the Matisse sketches—first time I have seen them. There are some so very beautiful and some I can hardly make out at all.

I forgot something—Saturday night I wore my new hat and coming home it started to rain. Laurie put the umbrella up and I grabbed the hat off and held it under the umbrella while the rest of us were out in the rain. I wouldn't have it spoiled for the world.

Now for Sunday afternoon! We went to the Lamoreux concert—Bauer played. We stayed for two Symphonies and Bauer and then beat it. I thought there was something wrong with me because I didn't enjoy it at all, but everybody else said just the same thing.

Yesterday afternoon Mrs. de Buyko and her daughter Mrs. Daunt and her daughter came in to tea. Also Mrs. Hyde and her daughter, who is a most very nice girl. It was the most exciting tea party I have ever seen—just like the mad tea party in Alice in Wonderland. First, there wasn't enough tea and I tried to make more by pouring a little hot water in each cup. Everybody looked polite—and hated it! Then I took the whole business out and Marie made some fresh. This time it was all right. But—I had left some of the cakes in the kitchen and forgot about them, and was perfectly furious because there wasn't enough cake. Harriet talked so fast and so hard to make up for the loss of food that I was about sure she would be worn out. But she wasn't.

Lots of love,

Sis

[The letter that follows was written by Sarah Stein to Sylvia's oldest brother.]

58 Rue Madame, December 6th

My dear Jeffrey:

As you expected Harriet came to me at once with Sylvia's problem, and I have been helping Sylvia for some time.

The problem is really not so much a question of this particular young man, but the question of Sylvia's whole mental attitude toward life. We have gone to the bottom of her tendencies, and she is now working to obtain an intelligent control of her thought in all directions through a higher understanding of what existence means. Naturally, she has had home-sick hours, but she is quite frank with me, and they don't last long. She has experienced a splendid physical healing, of which she has written to your mother. [The healing was of a migraine, which Mrs. Stein cured by teaching Sylvia to "rejoice."]

It is not important now whether she really tried her best to solve her problem according to what she knew of Christian Science when she was at home or not; she is trying to do so at present.

I can give no practical advice of any kind. I will say, however, that sincere effort to apply the teachings of Christian Science on the part of all concerned in this problem—in their attitude toward Sylvia, toward the young man, and toward themselves as an individual expression of Mind—as children of God—with all the qualities included in this real state of being—this sincere effort will help to solve matters in a way that no material steps—such as moving—ever can. Write to me whenever you feel so inclined.

Very sincerely yours,

Sarah Stein

December 8, 1912

Dear Family:

It is not time to write yet, but I shall begin this while I have a chance. We are sitting here in our nice warm salon—you know, we have the kind of a stove that never goes out. Harriet is reading and I ought to be practicing but can't because I just finished supper, and it is not good for one's voice to sing while chuck-a-block full. Ha-Ha!

This afternoon we took an open cab and drove for about an hour and a half in the Bois. It was a beautiful day—all kinds of sunshine—so all Paris was out. There was every kind of vehicle imaginable! From the very handsomest French cars down to bicycles—and numbers of everything. Then up overhead a monoplane was dancing around—just to kind of complete the scene. I was all dressed up in my new coat, furs and hat and looked quite handsome!

This morning we went to Church, of course! Everybody adored my costume. Its lovely to be able to afford so much pleasure to people.

Last night we went over to Steins. There were quite a number of people there. Some awful funny ones, but we don't talk to that kind, just sit and watch them while they look at the pictures. One very fantastic lady went all around the room with her lorgnette fastened first on one picture and then on another until finally they landed on me where they stuck. It was very funny. She just stood about six or eight feet away from me and looked—I suppose if I am not there next time she comes she'll take it for granted I've been sold. After the strangers left the friends all had tea, while Mike played the Victrola. They got some new records yesterday—some we haven't, and they are really quite fine. We left about 11:30. Guess that's why I'm a bit sleepy tonight.

Yesterday afternoon I went to tea at Mrs. Morrison's. There were about a dozen American girls there—very nice—most of them living here—few transient. I guess that's about all up to date.

Lots of love,

Sis

31 Rue de Vaugirard, Dec. 16, '12

Dear Grandma—

We have been having such lovely weather—
clear and not too cold and we have been out a
good deal.

You cannot imagine what a lovely city this is.
There are great open spaces with beautiful fountains and hundreds of lamposts with electric lights.
And the river is so pretty—spanned by handsome
bridges, so that it is a great pleasure to walk along
the sides of it and watch all the little steamers.

And the streets are crowded with people. In
front of the restaurants are little round tables three
feet deep—extending way out on the sidewalk
where hundreds of people are drinking coffee and
beer—even so late in the winter.

On Sunday afternoon we went across town to
see a collection of pictures that were to be sold at
auction today. They hung on the walls of an im-
mense room and hundreds of men were there examining them. Many were valued at $15,000, $20,000
and $30,000 a piece. The owner had collected them
over thirty years and had paid as much as $30 or
$40 for them. He had died, and the pictures were
being sold by the four sons. Up to date they had
brought at the auction $800,000. The paintings that
were the most valuable had been painted thirty or
twenty years ago by a man named Degas—who
had given them away to his friend or sold them for
a few dollars.

Well, while we were looking at the paintings an
old gentleman came in—a white bearded old man
of seventy or more. He wore a soft felt hat and a

rusty cape overcoat. He went from picture to picture examining each one carefully. Finally he lifted one from the wall to examine it more closely. A guard stepped up to him and said, "You mustn't touch the pictures." A man pulled the sleeve of the guard—"That's Degas"—he said. It was so interesting to see that old man, looking at his own pictures—for which dealers had come from every country and even from America—to the big sale today.

We spent last evening with Mr. & Mrs. Norledge—such lovely people. He used to be a Wall Street speculator, making as much as $100,000 a year. Now he and his wife have both become Christian Science practitioners.

People here wear many scarfs of beautiful fur and ermine scarfs and muffs are very commonly seen. I had my black coat made over, as it was very old fashioned in cut. Now it drapes to one side and has a gray fox collar. I wear it with a moleskin hat with my pretty white and black feather behind.

Do write me somebody about paradise feathers. There has been a mad run for them here this winter and the prices are beyond belief. I tried on a hat with a bunch of paradise the other day and asked the price. "$125" I was told. I never was so surprised. I tried another shop and was asked $95 for a little turban with a little bunch of paradise. Still I did not understand. Finally a milliner explained that this was an extraordinary year in that plumes were practically unused, and the price of paradise feathers had become "fantastic." They were selling for all prices from $50 to $100. Every hat is like a little turban with a fantasie straight up the back or up the front or shooting right out of the side.

There was a rich gentleman came to town last week from Philadelphia. He came over to collect pictures for a gallery that he was beginning to arrange for himself. He paid $10,000 for a small picture of Caisanne—a painter who had died practically unrecognized a few years ago, and since has become famous. *[It won't be long before Harriet learns to spell Cézanne's name correctly. During the 1920s she purchased several valuable portfolios of his watercolors.]* He dropped in on Sarah one Saturday night, fell in love with a painting of Picasso, for which Sarah had paid $55 six years ago—and offered $5000 for it, the painter having risen to great importance. Mike did not care to sell. *[The "rich gentleman" was Dr. Albert C. Barnes, whose collection would eventually be one of the finest in the United States.]*

Tomorrow I'm going into town to see the window displays for Christmas. They have all sorts of life sized mechanical figures.

Your loving

HARRIET

December 20, 1912

Dear Family:

Yesterday afternoon I walked just about all over Paris—for miles along the most wonderful river, and then to the zoo. I saw so many animals I have never seen before and of course was so muchly interested. I hate to say it but I really think I almost enjoy looking at animals better than museums. Ain't that an wicked thought to have in the land of art? Yesterday morning we rode in the country. I had a dandy little horse and the country was most extraordinarily beautiful! It had snowed the day before and everything was covered. There were some little boys making a snow man and I stopped to watch them they were having such a good time. We even had to stop every once in a while to dig ice out of the horse's hoofs. It was a wonderful morning. Wednesday I went across town to do some shopping—it looks so festive done up in its holiday clothes, and these merchants are so ingenious— they have such wonderful toys. All kinds of life-sized animals that do all kinds of things. I wish I could send a young menagerie home to the kids. How they would love the things!

Lots of love,

Sis

December 27, '12

Dear Family:

A great deal has happened since my last, in the way of Christmas excitement! First, we got so much mail from so many places—mail just kind of kept coming in all the time for three or four days. It was most wonderful! The books came from Ruth and I was so glad to get that Montessori book—I didn't know it was out. [In The Montessori Method, *published in 1912, the Italian educator Maria Montessori expanded on her theories. Sylvia was very much taken with Montessori's thoughtful approach to the education of very young children and hoped to apply it as a kindergarten teacher upon her return to California.*] When we were sitting here calmly and peacefully Christmas Eve all kinds of things came walking in—I got a lovely lace fissue thing from Alice and Harriet got a Spanish piece of pottery from Gertrude and Alice. Then we got cards—some awful pretty ones from people here. Christmas morning when I woke up I saw some peculiar snake-like thing on the floor and I was so startled I just sat up straight in bed and looked at it. It proved to be a blue silk stocking that Harriet had filled for me, with the most extraordinary looking things in it I have ever seen. She must have been collecting for days. The funny part was that the night before Harriet had come into my room, very quietly, long after I had gone to bed, and when I asked her what she wanted she said she wanted matches—the only thing she could think of—of course she expected to find me asleep—but, you know, nobody goes prowling around my room without waking me up. She tried to hang the stocking up but the blumin' thing wouldn't hang so she dropped it and ran. Then I had bought a back comb for Harriet an old Spanish affair which is most pretty—I took it in to give it to her and she screamed—she had bought a back comb for me—mine is carved ivory with a band of fancy gold thereon. Well, then we got to work fixing things up for the dinner—which, by the way, was a great success. Sallie and Laurie came in completely submerged in the most beautiful holly and a young Christmas tree. We had written limerics and joshes for each one. They were awfully good and everyone loved them. Here's the one they did on me:

"Oh! Oakland is a city
Which perhaps you may not know.
A right good place to come from

But an awful place to go.
Now Sylvia came to Paris,
A few months she would stay.
But she found she could sing
So her fancy took wing.
She decided she'd never go away.
When 'June is here' said Harriet,
'Toward Oakland we must steer'
Fair Sylvia shook her head and said,
'But think of my career!!'"

They gave me a cornet to go with it. The one I made for Harriet was a peach! You know the only thing in life she asks for is an "elimination of the non-essential"—you also know that Mike did all her shopping with her—for Christmas. Well, I set a doll up and had a little man in back of it, just laden down with bundles, big and small. Here's the verse:

At first she considered a husband,
And then she thought of a flat.
But since coming to Paris
She's done away with all that.
Of course they were not what she wanted
These things that she really hates.
She had come right here to Mikey—
Mike who eliminates.

Everybody loved it, but not nearly as much as I did. I wish I could think of the rest of them—they are so good. After dinner and all the excitement, we all went to Hyde's to the Christmas tree. The whole of our crowd of friends was there—the tree was the prettiest I have ever seen. They gave each one a present, Harriet got a pretty little plant, and I a very nice gold picture frame. They had much feed—tea, coffee, cakes, candies—beaucoup of everything. Mrs. de Buyko's granddaughter danced—Grecian—and then she sang. They played the Victrola which was a Christmas present, and altogether it was most nice and I loved it. We ate enough so that we didn't have to eat any supper.

I will try not to write about food any more, but you know it makes up such an important part of one's life I am sorry Grandma is not interested. I can describe food much better than Notre Dame or the Champs Elysee, anyhow.

Lots of love,

Sis

[Undated letter, marked "Private!"]

Dearest Ruth:

I have to write a letter home so won't tell you anything of what we are doing. But the chief reason for my having done this is to remind you that you are to let me know—<u>don't read this out loud to anybody</u>—how Mama is. I want to know always just how she is. *[Mama and Papa Salinger had just returned from a vacation trip to Honolulu. During the rest of Sylvia's visit to France there are frequent references to her parents' trips to various California resorts—recreational therapy for Mama.]* I am beginning to wake up now, and am just getting a smallest glimpse of what an idiot I've been to torture her so. I want also to ask you to do as much as possible for Mama—I mean in the way of making life pleasant for her, and maybe when I get home I will have enough sense to help out a bit myself. Please do it, let her have the comfort of the children and all—you know what I mean—And, please, let me know how <u>everything</u> is going at 911.

Lots of love,

S<small>IS</small>

January 2, 1913

Dear Family:

I got <u>eight</u> letters today—it was a record breaker. Much thanks, Jimmy, for all the rag. It was so welcome when it came walking in. Harriet and I had only spoken of it a few days before, saying how nice it would be to have some good old American rag-time. Thanks again—lots. The holiday weather has been marvellous! It usually snows on N.Y. day but, for our special benefit, it was glorious. Harriet and I took a walk in the Bois and along the Champs-Elyssees and it was a beautiful sight. The most interesting part of it all was the babies—I have never seen so many and so very good looking. They were all out, with their English or French nurses, which, by the way, are most picturesque, and they were so beautifully dressed. The children three and four all have their coats and hats trimmed in fur and then carry little muffs. Another feature of the walk was the beggars. You know, New Year's day is the biggest day of the year in France—so all the beggars in Paris, from every quarter, were out on the boulevards. Some women stood around with five or six children all sizes, helping them to beg. It was most sad.

I sent a programme to Papa—hope he got it. *[Among Albert Salinger's various real estate holdings in Oakland were buildings that housed silent movie theaters. Hence the "programme" and the frequent references in later letters to cinemas in Paris.]* That place is one in the quarter—I haven't been down town yet, but I know that there they cost three francs and two francs—according to the seats, and one franc upstairs. It was so funny when they showed an American cow-boy picture with all the sayings in French.

I am going to the dressmakers now to try on my violet dress. It is the most beautiful color you ever saw, and I am sure it will be a great success. I am going to have it trimmed in fur—what kind I don't know, the woman is getting it for me. Everything is trimmed in fur everywhere you go. It dresses up clothes so. Nicht wahr?

The voice is still a pretty little voice, so I have hopes. The other day when I came home with Victor Hugo's "Sing, Smile, Slumber" Harriet screamed. She said that you, Mama, used to sing it—but I do it in French!! I think I shall go back to my French teacher next week after having had two weeks vacation.

Lots of love,

Sis

[Harriet addressed the following letter to her oldest nephew.]

Paris, Jan. 2, '13

Dear Jeffrey:

Here are my drawings since I've arrived: Nov. 14, $430; Nov. 30, $300; Dec. 12, $275; Jan. 2, $200.

On my letter of credit I drew 80 pounds in New York. As to Sylvia's expenses—I am paying $20—over half of the household as I think that your father is having sufficient expenses (<u>This is not to be told to your father or mother.</u>) Now what I want to know is how far beyond these monthly expenses Sylvia is to go. For example, we thought of joining the Norledges in Nice for the last ten days of their visit, but I didn't know if Sylvia should incur the great expense of such a trip. It would possibly cost $100. And about clothes. Up to date she bought the set of furs for $106—a coat for $65—a hat for $16—1 dress for $25—and now she is getting another dress for $30. Is she to get only what she needs here or is she to get some things for home. Please get some definite information and let us know so that we may know where we are at.

I think Sylvia is getting attached to the people here. She has not yet heard from the Coffee boy but I shall be surprised if the letter disturbs her much.

I am off to the dressmaker with Sister—so goodbye and

lots of love,

HARRIET

January 6, 1913

Dear Fam:

I went to a sale this morning at Liberty's and the confusion of the whole thing has left me in such a muddle that I know I will never be able to write anything straight—but I'll try. The sale was very funny—the whole little Second Church was there—all our friends—everybody helping everybody else to pick out things. I got a couple of hats—each cost two and a half—one is a blue kind of velvet, very large and soft, the kind that you can twist any old way and that always looks pretty—the other, a smaller one that is very light, kind of mixed colors on top and light blue facing. It will make a good steamer hat and also a most comfortable motor bonnet. Then I got a little silk slip, kind of a kimono thing—it is a delight—mixed colors, red, brown, blue etc.—in the prettiest designs. I never saw anything quite so cute. I have it on now and adore myself.

Sunday noon Harriet was asked to lunch at Mrs. Morrisons—and I was not. They wanted Harriet alone! So I invited myself to Steins. After lunch we went to the Pantheon. I never know how really beautiful things are until I see them the third or fourth time. It is a marvel. I go rambling into the galleries and things now and just stay a little while instead of waiting for a day off. I adore my Lady of the Fan in the Luxembourg gallery. Every chance I get I go in and revel in her charms.

Saturday night was the most interesting gathering I have seen so far at the Steins. Such a mixture I have never seen. There was one woman from Australia, who paints—a man from England who is a consultant on most anything at all—people come from all parts of Europe for his opinion. He is a philosopher and, outside of that, just knows everything about everything! Then there were a couple of young English boys—about twenty, I think—Oh! so English! One is very interesting, a son of a disciple of Darwin—the other is a youth who comes of a very high English family and who is so brilliant he gives you a pain. Someone told us of how he had to take an exam in Greek art and hadn't done any work on it, so read two books through in fourteen hours. I overheard bits of his conversation with a lady what paints, and it was so stupid! Even I knew how stupid it was. Also, there was a man who is a sort of globe-trotter. He has lived a life-time in just about every city in the world. He is middle-age— and is not a <u>cat</u>. You can't mention a single place he hasn't been and doesn't know by heart. When he was introduced to me, he had heard of the Salingers in Oakland, knew immediately where I came from as soon as the name was mentioned. He is a psychic, by the way. Then there was another very nice young man who has been visiting in London for two months. He is French and since his long residence in London speaks Eng. quite well, and understands pretty nearly everything you say to him. He and I <u>discussed</u> Matisse. Get me? We spoke a little of Picasso also, but did not get back as far as the old masters.

Tonight I am entertaining a young man who has the reputation of staying till 'minuit' meaning mid-night, so I shall have to rest quietly all afternoon to be quite sure of not falling asleep. He does etching—supposed to be very good—from Chicago, alone in Paris etc. etc.—and he is very nice. I asked another fellow to come mit, but the mutt couldn't. I thought he might take Mr. Schneider home.

Lots of love,

Sis

Dear Family:

I took a walk across town this morning and climbed the tower of Notre Dame. It was a beautiful morning—all kinds of sunshine, so of course I enjoyed it immensely. I love being on top of things, anyway. I even had the extreme pleasure of hugging one of those horrible old gargoyles. I wonder if he will remember me next time I go up there. Also, the old bells are beauties—I was dying to ring one. But to stand up there and look out over Paris was such a pleasing sensation. The streets contain the most interesting variety of people—I don't suppose you can find that anywhere else. I watched them just for fun—all kinds of cabs—hundreds of them—loads of taxis, any number of carts being pulled by men—maids with loaves of bread at least five or maybe two feet long under their arms—nurse-maids with babies—handsome carriages and beautiful French cars. Then, way off in the distance, little pieces of regiments walking or rather marching through the streets. We could even see in the busy part of town the policemen stopping the traffic going in one direction to let the other—going across—get by. It is a good system and if Oakland continues to grow they will have to adapt it there. Altogether it was a most interesting experience. Its funny, they don't charge any regular price to go up, but you can give as much as you want—which means a few sous apiece. I almost forgot the river, its picturesque traffic—which is a very important part of the picture. We just watched the boats go under bridge after bridge steaming along the water. For all the traffic on the river, the whole time we were up there we heard one whistle. When we came down we went inside the place for awhile. Its the first time I have been there when there was no mass going on—and there were only about six people. It made it look so much larger, somehow. I love it more and more each time. It is glorious!

I just happened to think of what kind of suspence you must be in—because I remember having written in my last letter of the man who came to see me on Tuesday evening. He left at eleven fifteen instead of midnight, so I guess that there is something the matter with me as an entertainer, or maybe (just to cheer myself), someone put him wise, or I should say, reinformed him. He is very interesting—told me all about Montague Glass, who is a very good friend of his, how he is a Jew and his wife is not, and how the expression "lowlife" he got from his own father. Montie must be a very interesting person, from all accounts, not because he learned Low-Life from his father, but just all together. *[The Salinger family was devoted to the Yiddish dialect stories and plays of Montague Glass, creator of the well loved characters Potash and Perlmutter.]* Mr. Schneider is a very well known sketcher, is over here not to study but to work on his own hook and then he expects to take home works from here, for which there is a great demand in "the states."

Lots of love,

Sis

January 17, '13

Dear Fam:

About the Stein records—they have some marvels! I'll get a list and mark the best—I could get up a great deal of enthusiasm on the subject. They are sending to Germany and England right along for them, so, of course, will have the very finest—but I'm quite sure you can get them all home.

We went to a Cinema yesterday afternoon—holds about two hundred and fifty people—no day-light pictures, just one little electric light burning about the middle of the place—and it half concealed! The seats are arranged in rows of three on one side and four on the other—then they have the seats in the aisles which jump up when you get up, but which when occupied take up the entire isle. All the theatres here have the seats that jump up when you get up. Very good idea, no? The shows here all last two hours—This one cost three francs for reserved, which I looked for but could not find, and the rest two and one. A franc is twenty cents. This place is on one of the boulevards downtown and was full, but there was no one standing. They had an orchestra of piano, cello, and bass violin, which played the whole time, except during the five minutes intermission between shows—they probably have two shows in an afternoon. One stunt they work is season tickets—by which you save about two times or three, by going twelve—get me? Its rather complicated, I know. I'll get more information on the ticket dope for my next. The pictures are not nearly as clear as home, why I don't know, but they all seem kind of blurry. They had the Edison, Gaumont, Pathe—that's all I remember. Oh! yes, the place is long and narrow, has the entrance at one end, and one exit at the extreme other end—but no frame buildings. Enough of cinemas.

Harriet had a good dream the other night—in the form of a verse—

Heading was—
                    "Fatalism"
Verse was—
         "If I were you and you were me,
                We'd still be two and never three."
What think you of that? Harriet thinks the heading
the best part of it. Me thinks it is good. *[This couplet
is included in* I Love To Talk About Myself, *a collection of Harriet's verses, printed by the Grabhorn Press of
San Francisco in 1947.]*

I was just going to tell you about "Manon"
which we saw the other night, but happened to remember that Harriet did in her last letter. Harriet
doesn't think much of French operas, so, after this,
I am going with the Strauss family.

Jimmy, I want to tell you how much good your
rag time has done me. The other day I entertained
Mr. Frost by playing the whole repertoire through.
I was a wreck by the time I finished, you know, I
am a little bit out of practice, but it did the work,
anyhow.

The enclosed bit of gossip was in the Daily
Mail, which is printed in English here in Paris, and
whose editors have yet to be informed of the existence of such a place as San Francisco. *[The* Daily
Mail *clipping that Sylvia enclosed concerned a "joyous
demonstration" for the last horse-omnibus to run in
Paris. Meant to "signalize the complete triumph of the
petrol motor over the horse," the demonstration included
"150 motor-cars loaded with funeral wreaths" and between three and four thousand people. After much excitement, including military honors "rendered by a passing
regiment," the "historic demonstration, truly Parisian,
came to an end."]* I am sorry the old busses are gone—
it was great fun riding way up on top of them. The

automobile busses have no top—and they are so big they're just like street-cars.

Its half past three and I am going out to tea at four, and ain't even dressed. Mrs. de Buyko is coming in to have tea with Harriet. Wont it be funny when I get home and nobody gives me my customary 4:30 tea?

Lots of love,

Sis

January 21, 1913

Dear Family:

We went to the Cinema again last night! The blumin' show lasted for three hours. It was mostly all good, a couple of pictures, only, not being too first class, but the seats are so hard that after sitting there for that length of time, it was most difficult getting up. It is the one where they charge one franc. It was raining pretty hard—there were fifty people there—we counted 'em. The inside of the place is all painted white and the decorations are simply some palms, just a few, around the front and the sides. The orchestra is behind a curtain down in front. There is no exit besides the entrances, but instead of running deep into the building, the thing is built running parallel with the side-walk—I mean, the length of the theatre runs parallel with the side-walk. They only have Thursday and Sunday matinees, and one show a night. If you want moving picture statistics, give me a formula of questions and I will try to answer them, instead of this haphazard way of trying to tell you something about them.

Went over to the Louvre Sunday. I have never seen such mobs of people! Everybody in Paris is out on Sunday—they all go to the galleries, from the very richest down to the very poorest. We confined our day to the old Italian Masters—mostly all in one room—instead of just rambling through, looking around, as I usually do.

Took a long walk Saturday afternoon out to one of the Parks, which is so beautiful and green. Then we went out to the fortifications. It was most interesting seeing the gates of Paris and the wall. There is a road, or rather a boulevard that goes all the way around Paris. Sometime I am going to try to get to walk it. I don't know how far it is. I imagine somehow that it is a rather nice motor trip so when I walk it I guess I'll have to take a sleeping bag mit.

I've got a new plan—I am going to write one postal and one letter a week instead of two letters. What think you of that?

Lots of love,

Sis

[The first of these postcards follows.]

Jan. 24, '13

Dear Fam:

This is the once a week postal I told you about in my last. Went to hear Kreissler the other night—it was marvellous! never heard anything like it before. Harriet threatens to follow him from town to town but I am much too busy! Went riding yesterday—it was lovely—first day it was perfectly clear so I could see a good stretch of French country from the top of the hill—very nice!

Lots of love to everybody,

Sis.

31 Rue de Vaugirard (Why don't you ever use it?)

Dear Fam:

Harriet has gone on a lone trip to the Louvre. I hope she gets there this time, last time she got lost and got there just about closing time.

I had the time of my young life yesterday afternoon, when we went to see the "Little Duke." It is très, très charmant! The people who did it were perfect—the house was full, and it is such a pretty theater—the "Gaiety Lyric"—just about a comfortable size and so kind of homey. Between the acts everyone walked in the foyer and in the midst of the excitement Harriet decided she was hungry and swallowed a cup of coffee at the lunch counter. You should have seen her grab the last cake! After the performance we walked home, all the way across town. It was such a beautiful day and everybody in Paris walks around tea time. We visited one of the big grocery stores. It is a marvel! Such beautiful things so beautifully arranged. In the butcher department they had about a hundred pigs hanging up—in the back, then on the sides about the same number of legs of lamb, with fancy white paper background. But the prettiest thing is the way they have the sliced cold meats, in nice little oil paper envelopes—all ready to take home under your arm. Then the little shells with clams, and all kinds of shell fish chopped up and cooked like a entree. Oh! Gee! in the midst of all this I just remembered that you don't want to hear about eating any more. Better not read what I have written, then.

One of the best things that has happened to me here was Kreissler. It was a marvellous performance—I have never seen such an ovation given any one. The house went mad! After the last number they just sat there waiting for the encore.

I won't be able to finish this now. Company just arrived.

Lots of love,

Sis

Feb. 7, '13

Dear Family:

Tuesday was Mardi Gras and the streets were packed jammed with people in mask and throwing confetti. The law doesn't permit any of the awful noise things we have at home. I didn't go across town, but I did walk thro the Luxembourg Gardens. It was a wonderful day and the children looked charming in their little costumes. They wore the things of all centuries, as far back as you could ever imagine, and threw confetti at each other and were perfectly adorable! Some of them were just old enough to toddle, but they were dressed up too and threw confetti just like everybody else. The most interesting part of it was that the costumes all fit perfectly, so you see how seriously the French Mothers consider their children's pleasure. There is a secret somewhere in this country of the bringing up of happy children. I shall try to find out what it is—I have seen about two children cry since I have been here, and I see a great many of them because they are always out in the gardens—I mean the Luxembourg gardens. After walking through the gardens I went to tea at Miss Miller's—she is a very nice girl from the south. *[Rachel Miller is destined to play an important supporting role as the drama continues. But Sylvia's geography is a bit off—Miss Miller was from Philadelphia.]* Miss Hyde and Sallie Strauss were there also, and we sewed. Tuesday night the Norledges came in—their sister was visiting them from England, and she came mit. They are just the very nicest couple I have ever known, or ever hope to know. I don't think any two people could be more beautiful thro and thro than those two. They are the readers, you know, and they read just as beautifully as they are beautiful.

Wednesday afternoon Harriet and I went downtown to see the Saint Chapel. It has the most beautiful interior of any church in these regions—it took my breath away—It is marvellous, looks like one enormous jewel. We take a guide book along now, just like tourists, and it makes everything so much more interesting. From there we went into the hall of justice. It is one of the old palaces, you know, and is so beautiful. In the ante-chambre the lawyers all promenade, between cases—they wear the cap and gown and are very imposing looking. We went in to hear one case, but it was too intimate for us so we left. It was all kinds of awful family troubles—then we went into another, where they were having a trial because a man was run over by an automobile. I don't know whether the lawyer was pleading for the chauffeur or against him, and I don't even know whether it was the man who was on trial for being run over. Anyhow, I have to learn a little more French before I try that stunt again. I wanted to see the trial of the Automobile bandits, but you can't get in without a ticket.

The weather has been so marvelous that I am quite sure spring has come. The river is way up and looks beautiful! All traffic thereon has been stopped—they can't get past the bridges. I went riding yesterday morning and the country was too wonderful for words. In the afternoon I walked the streets of this wonderful city. I am just beginning to wake up to its grandeur—and love it all.

Last night Mr. and Mrs. Morrison were in to dinner. He is a artist and she does some kind of theatre connection work. Tonight Mildred is coming in.

Everybody write lots.

Lots of Love,

Sis

February 11, 1913

Dearest Ruthie:

Thanks! I was glad to get your letter. Most glad to know Mama is so very well. Sallie is fine—expects her baby in about two weeks. The little community are looking forward with much interest to the great event. About travelling, I don't know just why I should! There seems to be a great deal to see and do in Paris—enough to keep one busy for years, instead of months. But, Harriet is going to ask Mama about it, and, if she wants us to travel—very well, then. And you want to be informed about me. Well, its rather hard to say just where I am. I don't know. I am all right as long as I stay here, but of course, could not attempt going home yet—that's the way I feel about it now. I mean that I don't feel the frightful loneliness that never left me for the first month or so—hardly at all any more. I am really happy here now, that's one of the reasons it seems so kind of silly to break away and travel. My peace of mind seems rather more important at this particular time. Of course, I would like to know how things are going with the various people concerned—but, I suppose that's not possible. You know what I am doing—working <u>very hard</u> with Science—practicing about an hour a day—taking two lessons a week—also three French lessons a week with work in between. The people we see most of are the Steins, next the Strausses. Then there are two ladies, Miss Morton, who used to be a trained nurse in S.F., but has given it up for Paris—Miss Miller, who lost all her people at home and came over here to study singing. They are both very nice people. Then the Hydes, about whom we seem to write often. Mr. and Mrs. Morrison—she is lovely!! Mrs. de Buyko and her daughter Mrs. Dent—Mr. and Mrs.—Norlidge (I always spell it wrong.) Mr. Bochet, a young fellow interested in music and art—he is great fun and very alive. *[The funny, lively Chicago-born Main Bocher would later achieve international fame as a couturier—after glamorizing his name to Mainbocher.]* Mr. Schneider—interested in sketching—Mr. Frost who used to paint but now does nothing—not too exciting! Mr. Bochet expects to settle for awhile in N.Y. when he goes back, so I am going to give him a letter to Gurden. That's all I can think of now, but I know there are lots more. Any more information you de-

sire, just let me know—and, any information you
may possess—kindly convey same.

Lots of love,

Sis

Dear Family:

Saturday night I went to the much-talked of
Opera house—with Max Rosenberg and his cousin,
and the two Heyman sisters one of whom is living
here. *[Harriet was delighted by the arrival of Mr. Rosenberg, a friend of the Stein family from San Francisco. She
and Sylvia would now have an escort so they could, as
she said, "go anywhere at night."]* We had a loge and
were very swell. Lohengrin was very beautifully
done and I loved it all. Of course the house is magnificent! We walked in the foyer between acts and it
was all very wonderful. After the Opera we went to
Montmarte to one of the popular cafés. It isn't like
home—nobody ever gets drunk. I think that is why
the jollity all seems so inoffensive. They gave away
big balloons—toy ones, and little celluloid balls,
which everyone proceeded to throw at everyone
else. The women are all so beautiful, and nothing
out of the way took place at all. The orchestra never
stops at all—really—they have to keep up a steady
fire of music—and they played all the old rag things,
that I played home. Everybody sang—they all know
them. There were a few tourists—but most of the
people looked like regulars. Such handsome American and English young men, probably living here.

65

Well, I'm glad I got that out of my system—don't have to go there any more. We left at <u>2</u>!

Last night I went to see Sarah Bernhardt as Queen Elizabeth—for 1 franc. It was a beautiful picture—she is a marvel! There was a woman in back of us who refused to take off her hat when the woman in back of her asked her to. She just sat there perfectly calm and peaceful and said that she was bald and seventy and didn't see why that shouldn't be reason enough. When the manager requested her to remove her chapeau she said she would not and it would take four men and a corporal to put her out etc. It was most entertaining—having been done in such a pleasant spirit.

Well, the sun is shining and I am going out to take a look at Paris.

Lots of love,

Sis

March 7, '13

Dear Family:

If I have figured rightly, you got all the letters explaining the whys and wherefores of our staying until Fall. *[These letters are missing.]*

Last night was a very exciting evening. First, I expected Mr. Bochet, and when the bell rang almost fainted on the spot to see great big Mr. Morrison in to pay a call on Harriet. Well, Mr. Bochet and I disappeared into the dining room and left Harriet and her unexpected caller in the salon. About eleven o'clock there was a mysterious knock on the door and Mrs. Morrison came in for her husband—she had been at a meeting. About fifteen minutes after that there was another knock and Allen Stein came in to bring something of Harriet's from the Steins. It doesn't sound exciting to tell about, but it sure was. This morning Laurie came in at about half past eleven and donated a lesson to me. He dropped in to lunch and Harriets not being there thought he would take that time in giving me a little lesson—very nice of him. Nicht wahr? Sallie is still at the hospital—Her baby is adorable and she is perfectly fine! She is thinking of coming home Sunday and I am to go out and carry the baby for them. I can't wait for Sunday!

Yesterday afteroon I went to visit the Pantheon. It was the first time I have had a real good light, so I feel that I saw the paintings for the first time. It is all so lovely! After which, I went to a cinemato-graph and saw a few very good pictures. I don't write about the Cinemas any more now. I'm waiting for your list of questions, Papa.

Wednesday I went to the Clunie to take an-other look at the tapestries. I think they are mar-vellous! just stood there and looked at them for an hour. I came home from the Clunie and lay down for a few minutes and fell asleep—slept for three hours—what think you of that? And, Miss Miller came in to dinner, and hasn't quite recovered from the shock of my sleeping in the afternoon. I haven't either. But the point is they had to wake me up when she came. The other night Harriet and I went to dinner with Max Rosenberg. We went to a café at Montemarte—such a nice, comfortable, pretty place. The walls are painted with various happy scenes, one they said was worth 30,000 francs. It is such a nice place to go—all nice looking people there, and its big and roomy and very light—most of the cafés give one the impression of not having enough room.

Tonight Mr. Rosenberg is coming in to dinner and I am going with him to visit Mr. and Mrs. Cooper—a young couple from San Francisco. He is supposed to be a wonder pianist—is studying with Bauer. So, I am anxious to hear him play. I can't remember if I told you about the Kreissler concert last Sunday. He played the Beethoven Concerto and he <u>played</u> it! That man is a wonder. It was the regular Colonne symphony and he was the soloist. I'd walk ten miles to hear him play ten minutes.

No more now.

Lots of love,

Sis

March 11, 1913

Dear Family:

We received a lovely letter from Mama and Papa yesterday. No, Mama, I did not pay $60.00 for a hat—it was $16.00. Feel better? Harriet has a kind of way of mixing up francs and dollars and not always coming out right. I have one evening dress now, and shall probably get another before I come home.

Last night we went to see the Walkyrie at the Opera House. Max Rosenberg took us and Miss Miller and we sat in the second row balcony, in those wonderful big roomy armchairs and had a beautiful time. The thing was splendidly staged and very well sung. The chief fault was that it was done in French. I like German so much better for

Wagner. We prominaded in the foyer in the good old way and I loved it all. There weren't very many beautifully gowned women, but enough to make it pleasant. After the Opera we went to one of the swell cafés and had a wonderful chicken salad. Harriet said it was. Everywhere in the cafés they play American ragtime.

By the way, Theresa Ehrman is coming over I think soon, so will you communicate with her right away, and if she has any room anywhere ask her to bring a big box of Lehnhardt's chocolates. *[Therese Ehrman, Sally Strauss's sister, had lived with the Michael Steins between 1903 and 1905. She will be an impressive supporting actress as Sylvia's drama proceeds.]* Please please please. It doesn't sound like anything, but candy is so expensive here we never get any, and anyhow, there is nothing like Lehnhardts. It doesn't matter if it gets stale—it will be wonderful, just the same. Also, Harriet wants some tea—ours is just about giving out—not necessarily that frightfully expensive stuff, but some Oolong. Also, three or four tubes of Boradent tooth-paste. I think it would be wise to ask her right away as she will probably leave very soon. Please do it!!! It will mean so much!

Last Saturday I took my lesson in the morning, went to lunch with Laurie Strauss and then we went out to bring Sallie and the Baby home from the hospital. I feel like an old old experienced mother next to them. I carried the baby home, helped them get about settled (the nurse didn't come till the next morning)—and you should have seen the excitement! Then I came home and found Harriet so lonely, she had been alone all day, and didn't think much of it. Sunday afternoon we went to the Art Decorative to look at some of Mr. Bochet's things he displayed and then we went upstairs in the Louvre to see the old furniture—it is all so lovely—I had never been there before.

This afternoon we are going to tea at Mrs. de Buyko's so I have to quit now and practice. Please remember about Theresa!

Lots of love,

Sis

March 17, 1913

Dear Family:

Yesterday, having been Sunday, I celebrated by going to Sallie's to lunch and bumming around just about all over Paris with Laurie. First I stayed with the baby for a while to let Sallie go out for a walk. He is the loveliest baby and so remarkably good. But I lost out—because, Harriet went with the Steins out to Matisses place to see all his new things he just brought home. Saturday Harriet and I went to the Louvre, in the Egyptian part—which I have never seen before. All the old casket things beautifully carved etc.—then into the rooms of the first Italian paintings. There is always so much to see there, in the Louvre, but as much as I see, I always run back to take a last look at the Winged Victory, whom I worship! It closes at four, so we rambled over into the Tuillerie gardens and sat there for a while watching some people feeding the sparrows. They fly right up and eat out of one's hand. After which bit of recreation we went out to the Café Marigny to tea. It is really a theatre, where they have plays and concerts and things, but in the afternoon it is turned into a café—I mean, the foyer is a café where you are served at little tables up against the wall, and where they have people in street clothes dancing. They ragged, just like in S.F. Also they did the tango—a new exaggerated rag, with loads of very attractive extra steps in it. It is a new dance here, and it seems that everybody's doin' it. Are they home? After that we walked down the boulevard toward Napoleon's tomb, when it was just about getting dusk. It is all so wonderfully lovely!

Friday night we spent at the Morrisons. Its terrible how I always want to laugh at that man—and really, you know, he isn't so awful funny. But he is so English!!! and his wife saves the situation always by being so decidedly American. Harriet never dares to look at me while he is talking—it would mean disgrace for life. Thursday night Harriet and I went to Gertrude's. We had such fun—just giggled until very near two o'clock, when we decided to run home. They live just a block away—its wonderful Gertrude Stein is doing a great deal of writing now, some of her things having been on exhibition at the Post Impressionist exhibition in New York. It was such fun listening to her discussing probable publishers etc. *[Three Lives had been published, by the Grafton Press, in 1909; Gertrude's next major publication,* Tender Buttons, *didn't appear until 1915.]* She is a picnic, and Alice is so very sweet. I almost forgot—we had some Oregon apples at Alice's—My! they were good!

Thursday afternoon I went to see a collection of Renoir paintings, on display at one of the big dealers places. It was so beautiful. He is the man who has been painting for about forty-five years, is now in his eightys—still working, turning out marvellous stuff every day—all this with a hand deformed with rheumatism. It is said of him that he has never painted anything sad. The display I saw was just one burst of joy!

Wednesday night after service we went to Steins for a little concert—meaning victrola—the Coopers were there and Mr. Bergdorf of Carmel and S.F., who is very nice. He paints also—has been to Holland and Egypt and various places and is going home by way of China and Japan. He and I talked Carmel until I could almost see the ocean before me.

Write lots now because it is Spring and more steamers are coming in all the time—carrying mail.

Lots of love,

Sis

March 25, 1913

Dear Family:

About the pictures, Mama, I am not thin! not in the least, don't see where you ever got that idea from. I thought they were so fine—as I said to Harriet—I never knew before—I was pretty. It is now a quarter after three—I have six girls coming in to tea, and Harriet is down town, also Marie is out. But, if they come before I am ready for them, they'll just kind of have to wait. We are going to see Isadora Duncan dance tonight, and I am really most excited about it. It is in the Trocadero, too, a place I haven't been to yet. *[Unfortunately we do not have Sylvia's reactions to Duncan and the Trocadéro. But we do have the program, which she saved. Mlle. Duncan and her pupils from the Darmstadt School of Dance performed to the*

Orpheus *ballet and choral music of Gluck, with the assistance of Mounet-Sully of the Comédie Française, Rodolphe Plamandon of the Opéra, and the Colonne chorus and orchestra under the direction of Gabriel Pierné.]* Last night Mildred was in to dinner. She is so remarkably interesting! We were talking about Ellen Terry and when she called her Nell—it seemed so strange to me. It's like a different world. Margaret Anglin has been in Paris and Mildred told us all about going shopping with her and all. *[Margaret Anglin (1876– 1958) was an American actress with a long and important career.]* It was such fun. Yesterday afternoon I went out to Matisses. I think Harriet has told you about the place. It is so beautiful! Mrs. Matisse is charming! I was so surprised. Mr. wasn't home. We saw everything, from his studio down to the pet monkey. We had tea on the lawn, too. And I am so proud, I understood very nearly everything they said. Its wonderful to really begin to be part of a French conversation. It was a fete day and all the people of Paris were out picnicing—they don't get drunk here like they do home—so its fun watching them. They just eat! and have such a simple good time—real "menchlich" [*homey*] like—you understand.

Sunday, being Easter, I went to Notre Dame. It was a beautiful ceremony, but it seemed to me it should have been much more impressive. The Cardinal, with his bishops and things around him, all magnificently robed, walked up and down the isles, blessing all the people—and the infants in arms, the children and even the grown ups kissed his ring—it signifies something, I don't know just what, but I consider it most unsanitary. The music was lovely! a big boy choir and a tenor who had some voice. Notre Dame was crowded! Just imagine the mob! We were upstairs in the place that is only open for big occasions. Also, they played the organ, which is only for big occasions.

I forgot to tell you that out at Matisse's yesterday I saw a dirigible—the first one I've seen. It was a beautiful sight—I'm so glad I saw it.

Saturday we took the boat up the river to St. Cloud—it is the place where there used to was a castle but it burned down. There is a big cultivated park, and then woods, for miles. Its all green now and is so lovely! From the site of the castle you can see Paris in the distance with the towers looming up. It was a beautiful view—and such a clear day. We came back on the street car because we thought it went along the river—instead of which it went through a lot of funny little towns. But it was a lot of fun, riding way up on top of that bumpy little thing—Its just like the kind you see in the moving pictures home.

Lots of love to everybody,

Sis

April 4, 1913

Dear Family:

We had a dandy ride yesterday, out in the country, all in blossom and green and an airship floating over us. It was beautiful. But have I told you, I made the discovery that I don't know how to ride at all! I used to think I was an wonder, but no more. I can't do the work on an English saddle. I never would have believed it if anyone had told me. I am not a good horse-woman at all!! It hurts to have to make the confession, but its only too true.

However, Mr. Stein is teaching me so maybe by the time I get home I'll know how to ride really.

Theresa is expected tomorrow, so every body is most excited. Have I told you the Strausses have taken an apartment just a few doors from us and Theresa is going to live with them? Its wonderful— The Steins and Strausses and us all in about a block. Also, have I told you we are all going away together this summer, to a little place on the border of France and Spain, where there is the most loveliest surf bathing—I already have two pupils—that is, if the waves aren't too big. If they are, I shall have to be a pupil myself. *[Sylvia had taught swimming the previous summer at the University of California women's pool. A memorable snapshot shows her waving at the camera, oblivious to the fact that she is holding her pupil's head face-down in the water.]* The Steins, Strausses, Theresa, Miss Miller, probably the whole family of Hydes and us. Won't it be fun? I am most excited about it. Then I will be able to go right on with my singing, having Laurie with me, and with my French, having Allan with me. Everything just comes out fine, the further we get along—Miss Miller studies with Laurie, too, and we have such fun together.

Would you want me to bring home some records that you can't get over there? There are a lot of German ones that are wonders—also some from England. The duty wont be much, and they can be very carefully packed and put in the bottom of the trunk. I am sure it would be worth while. And, besides, I think they are a good deal cheaper than the fine ones at home, even with duty.

We went to the opening night of the new theatre Wednesday night. It was a beautiful sight. The most beautiful audience I have ever seen. And how they cut—my—oh! my! clear down to the waist-line in back, V shape—and in front, oh, well, most anywhere. The attraction of the place, however, was Isadora Duncan who had a loge along with some others, and who is so very lovely—from a distance. Afterward I went up to her to look her straight in the face and saw the most peculiar make-up ever—all kinds of funny black lines—it was horrible! But she is lovely from a distance. Between numbers, when everyone promenaded, she was standing just at the door of her loge, talking French to seven men. I sat with my glasses glued to her the whole time.

The music was not terribly interesting, to me— but it was fun seeing the men. You know, they played all modern music, and the composers lead their own stuff. *[At the Inaugural Concert of the Théâtre des Champs Élysées, which was "dedicated to French music," the orchestra was conducted by Camille Saint-Saëns, Gabriel Fauré, Vincent D'Indy, Claude Debussy, and Paul Dukas.]*

I forgot to tell you something about the new theatre—the orchestra seats are all big arm chairs, with enough room between the rows that people can pass you comfortably while you sit as if in a drawing-room. Each chair has its own arms—get me? It is a wonderfully comfortable place.

Alice tells me that Clarence has a job with the electrical something or other of the Panama Exposition. It sounds good.

And I never told you about the horse-show! My, oh my! I had such a most wonderful time! I went with Mr. Stein, Leo Stein, Mr. Rosenberg and Allan. How's that for a bunch? Well, they had all kinds of drills first, of men who are trying out for the cavalry. It gave us a very good idea of the training system, but the riding was atrocious! Then they showed the officers who had had an endurance run the day before—they gave a prize to the man who brought his horse in in the best condition, after having covered the greatest ground. They all looked in splendid condition. There was team work jumping—it was lovely, first singly, then in twos and so on, up to sixteen jumping together. The best thing of the whole day was the officers who all have high-schooled thorough-bred horses—They were beauties! One of them looked, and parked, and reared just like Pesos—I know Papa will appreciate the reference. *[Pesos was Sylvia's own beloved riding horse, purchased for her by an indulgent father.]* I didn't take my eyes off of him the whole time. He had all the same markings, same color, and carried himself just the same. It was wonderful seeing them fifty all at once, rearing and finally parking all around in figure eights and circles and things. I stood for three hours and was so excited, never even knew I was standing. It was cavalry day! I think I shall go again before it closes.

Lots of love,

Sis

April 8, 1913

Dear Family:

A lot of exciting things have happened lately, but nothing nearly so exciting as receiving Lehnhardt's candy. Harriet thought maybe Theresa would bring it, but I never hoped for one minute, and when it came walking in, I danced seventeen jigs. I don't think I have ever been as glad to see anything as I was to see the name on top of the box. It was a joyous moment—and it is so good! I am so glad Harriet had a birthday and so grateful to the nephews for remembering that it was Lehnhardt's that she likes. The next exciting thing was the arrival of Theresa. She came at three in the morning! We met the Strausses in front of a café after theatre, looking so dreadfully sad—it was because Laurie had just phoned and found out the hour. I wanted to stay and go down with him, because Sally had to go home to the baby, but Harriet wouldn't hear of it. Anyhow, the Steins were there to meet her and everything went off fine! I saw her for a minute yesterday and she is beautiful! They move Saturday, and are going to leave the baby here with me all day. I am so excited about it.

We went to a Beethoven festival at the new theatre Sunday night and it was lovely—The new leader, Felix Weingartner, is a wonder. Paris is crazy about him—he is very young, so good-looking and a smile that would make any body play well. Lilli Lehmann sang—she is so pretty—her hair is snow-white, and she looks very much like Grandma in her sweet moments. She is probably about sixty-five, very stately, very simply dressed, and such a gracious, friendly manner. The house went mad over her.

The audience was very interesting—near us sat a woman who was the most aristocratic looking person I ever saw, and such a pearl collar, my, oh, my! There are always a lot of Dukes and Duchesses and things, so I guess she was one of them. And, Isadora Duncan was there again, in the most prominent loge in the place. When she came in every eye in the place watched her. They all stood up and just looked. She was dressed in white, with an ermine coat that covered her all up—such an coat!

Yesterday afternoon Harriet and Mrs. Nordlege and I went down to Jean Halle to see about Harriet's dress. While she was fitting it, I sat outside and watched the parade of models. They are wonders. They have a walk, commonly known as the "model glide" (by me, only) and how they do it! The gowns were, of course, most extraordinary, in the sense of there being so little of them, and also in the sense of their magnificence, but the ladies in them were the attraction. They were enough to make you want to buy the whole place. The woman asked me if I didn't want to look at some "jeune fille" dresses, they have such chic ones. A model came gliding along in one simple little afternoon frock of blue. The lady thought it would be "charmante" for mademoiselle—but mademoiselle most ungraciously asked the price—only $110—not francs. I just said "not today" and beat it. Everybody laughed.

I am going down town now with Harriet to ramble on the wonderful boulevards a bit. So, this is all for now.

Lots of love,

Sis

April 14, 1913

Dear Family:

I got a postal from Albert Elkus tonight. [A *nephew of Sylvia's brother-in-law Charles Elkus, Albert was another of her ex-suitors. He later achieved some success as a composer and considerable success as an edu-*

cator, serving for many years on the faculty of the music department of the University of California at Berkeley.] He is coming over in June to study with Bauer, who teaches for June and July. It will be nice having him here. Max Rosenberg leaves this week for home and I asked him to call at 911 which he will do, undoubtedly. I am sure you will all like him.

Theresa is here, living with the Strausses just a few doors from us. They moved last Saturday, and I kept the baby for them all day. He is an angel!

This afternoon we went to an exhibition of Matisse's latest works. They are almost all the same as I saw in his studio but now they are framed and hung they look so different. An old man, great big heavy fellow with such a jovial face, came in and took one look at a woman's head, a sculpture of Matisses, and went out in roars of uncontrollable laughter. We all screamed—it was so funny. After spending about an hour there we went down to one of the cafés on the boulevard and had an ice, sitting on the outside, watching the people. It was fun. After that, we went to another exhibition—one of the bunch of post-impressionists who think themselves as fine at Matisse. It was remarkable to see the difference between all those men and the other man.

Sunday I went to the finals of the horse-show. It was an exhibition of cross-country hurdles— about forty horses taking part. It was very interesting. Then they had some high-jumping—the horse who won the high jump did it in nine feet—get that? He is about twenty-five years old and his front legs are all bandaged and wiggly. He can hardly walk, but how he can jump. I think I would have enjoyed it much more if he didn't have bunged-up legs.

Harriet is sitting here discussing all the places we might be travelling to next month so I am getting worn out. In the last fifteen minutes we have been to England, Holland, Spain, Italy—and I don't know where else. But in all probability we will go somewhere very soon. Doesn't that sound satisfying?

I have to go now, so aurevoir—

Loads of love,

Sis

Paris, Apr. 28, '13

Dear Family:

I am sitting here in the Luxembourg gardens, with my tan coat and linen dress of last year on, and am slowly but quite surely roasting to death. We are having the most marvelous weather—just like the middle of summer. I wish you could see the crowd here—there are at least one hundred babies in sight—women are doing their mending and darning, and men are smoking and reading. It is a wonderful place. The woman just came to collect the two cents for the chairs and I couldn't display the tickets, because Sally ran off with them, but I explained it to her and she beat it—saved four cents!

Harriet is off for the day, entertaining Mr. and Mrs. Herman Hering, the man who gave a C.S. lecture here last night. Harriet was on the entertainment committee, but don't worry, Grandma, the church paid for it. For Heaven's sake don't read that to Grandma, but it just kind of slipped out.

Last Friday we had the most wonderful time,

but I want to tell you about something funny that happened before I tell you about Friday. We drove to the Bois in a cab the other day, and wanted to go to one of the places out there to tea. We told the cocher to drive there and he said "Mais, c'est très cher." How we laughed! I guess we didn't look it somehow. Then when we came out of the place, and all the limousines were calling for their various owners, our old broken down cab came up and we were assisted by just as many people as the limousine owners were—to our carriage. It was all very amusing. The place is one of the most interesting I've been to here—so many beautiful women— most beautifully grand! And it is always so funny to see, in the midst of all the glory, a few open-mouthed, open-eyed tourists, like us. Then there was a young girl who had just come from a first communion—she looked so out of place in her white gown and veil. It was an interesting performance all through. Now for Friday! Theresa and Harriet and I took an early train and went down to Chartre. It is beautiful old town—seemed small, but they say it has 25,000. We went first to the cathedral, which was built in the 13th century. I think I like it better than Notre Dame, but it is hard to say—it is so different. In the cathedral, we climbed up to the bell tower and at twelve o'clock the keeper rang the bell with us standing right on top of it, or rather, on the scaffold that holds it—and he rang it ninety times!! The bell is so big that ten people can stand inside of it comfortably. Can you imagine what a noise it made? Well, we recovered sufficiently to climb down again after seeing the most wonderful view of the entire surrounding country. And it is nice seeing the architectural structure from above—you get a much better idea of it. Also, being right close to outside of the stained glass windows, which, by the way, are the most beautiful I have ever seen. The one in the front of the cathedral is a marvel of color and beauty. Well, we left the cathedral and went down town to lunch. We had been recommended to the Hotel D'Angleterre and I ran all over the blumin' town looking for it. But, after much searching, we went into the Hotel de France and decided it was very good—afterward we found out that was the place they meant. It seems that the three or four hotels of Chartre are working against each other to see which one can get the foreigners, so we profited. I never in my life ate so much—they just kept piling it on—all for three francs. I wish I could remember all we had—I am sure it was ten courses. Well, after lunch (?) we went back to the cathedral for another look—it was even more beautiful than the first time. We stayed there awhile and then took a walk down along the river. The women were doing their washing—just like in the moving pictures—and you ought to have seen the old, old women just scrubbing away to beat the band—and they do get the clothes white—really snow white. The town is so picturesque with all the little crooked streets and tumbled-down houses. The swell part of town is all along the river—and each house has a beautiful big garden and a private laundry—with all the washing done in the river. Its wonderful. After trotting around the town, we finally landed back at the cathedral—took a last look and hit for home. It was such a wonderful day.

Loads of love,

Sis

Dearest Ruthie:

Don't address any more letters here to the apartment because we are thinking of giving it up on the first of June to go to Spain. At last, we have some definite plans. We are going to the Chateau district for about a week, week after next, I think. Then, about the first of June we are going to Spain for a month and then meet the Steins, Strausses etc. at a summer resort on the border of France, where they are going to spend a couple of months. After that it gets a bit indeffinite again, but I think we shall probably go to Germany before coming home—by way of England. I think that's almost enough to see of Europe this time. Don't you? We shall probably sail some time after the fifteenth of October because the winter rates go on then. It all sounds so handsome.

We heard Melba and Kubelik in concert the night before last—If Melba had been about twenty years younger and Kubelik had been Kreissler it would have been a splendid performance—but—I can't find a trace of Melba's voice. It is all kind of raw and squeaky. She is very charming, however—exceedingly fat, but most marvellously gracious.

I am going to the dressmaker now, am getting a little summer dress to bum around in. We have been to every store in Paris (almost) trying to get a few things for summer, ready made, but its impossible, can't get a thing. So, I went back to my old dressmaker who made all my winter things. Then, I am going across town to get seats for Tristan and Isolde for Monday night. Tuesday night we are going to the Bach Passion Music—St. Matthew. I heard it once when I first came over, and am very anxious to hear it again. It is marvellous! Then, I am going this week to a production of the Barber of Seville which is supposed to be very grand. Mignon Nevada, daughter of Emma Nevada, made her debut in it last night at the new theatre, and Paris is quite crazy about her. *[Emma Nevada (1859–1940) was an American-born operatic and concert soprano.]* In June, the whole troupe of Russian dancers are coming for about fifteen performances—but I don't know whether we will be here for it or not. There are always so many big things happening all the time, its impossible to even try to see them all.

The country is lovely now—between showers. We leave home in our furs, armed with an umbrella, and by the time we get across the boulevards we see the sun shining and all the beautiful ladies in their spring clothes. It is most awful distressing.

Lots of love,

Sis

May 9, 1913

Dear Family:

We have been shopping lately, trying so hard to get something to wear—and it is such a job here. You have to have everything made—nothing good comes ready-made at all. I succeeded in almost ordering a coat yesterday, but the woman wanted to get a better color cloth, so I shall finish ordering it Tuesday. The hardest work I have done in a long time was yesterday when I went down to get the seats for the Russian Ballet which is coming soon for a series of ten performances. It was the second day of the sale and when I got there almost a quarter after eleven, the box offices having opened at eleven, there were three offices, with three lines, each line containing about twenty-five people. It was a wonderful thing—how I ever got the seats, I don't know, but I did—and they are very good. The tickets, orchestra seats, for the first night of each performance, for instance, the first night of the ballet, the first night of each opera (Russian) there are three operas—the tickets are fifty francs—(ten dollars) what do you think of that? then the 10% besides for the poor—which is charged in every theatre here. We are not going on the first nights—the other nights are thirty francs (6 dollars)—and we are not going in the orchestra either. I didn't tell you the prices to tell you how much money I am spending, but just because I want to show you how Paris goes plumb crazy when anything extraordinary comes along—and will pay any price at all. We are going to the dances twice and to one of the operas—"Boris Godonnow."

Harriet and I are planning to take a two or three day trip to Rouen—a cathedral town about four hours out of Paris—we are going tomorrow morning, if it doesn't rain. Miss Miller is going with us. Then the Norledges are going out to a little town in the woods somewhere, and want us to come down with them a few days, which little thing I am most anxious to do.

While I think of it, I want to tell you, Papa, that you need not worry about my spending any money buying things you wouldn't approve of. I can see by your letters that you are scared. I never buy anything at all—the only money I spend is for concerts and operas, and that I consider part of Paris. I have

to get some clothes now, because it is beginning to
be just a bit too warm for my corduroy. But, really,
you can take my word for it, I never buy anything
at all. I haven't even as much here in the way of
clothes and things as I always have at home. Feel
Better?

I didn't know how much I loved it here until we
came so kind of near to going home—that is, before
your cable came—If you could only come—I have
an idea—have Ruth and Chip stay at 911 for a few
months and you, Mama and Papa take a run over
here. It would be so wonderful. Better consider it—
I have to take a bath now, so

Loads of love to everybody,

Sis

May 16, 1913.

Dear Family:

I had hysterics in seventeen different languages when I got Mama's letter telling us about
pesach—we never even knew it was at all! Don't tell
Grandma! *[The Salingers were quite thoroughly assimi-
lated by 1912—but Grandma Levy remained staunchly
Orthodox. She observed the holidays—such as Pass-
over—and in the new house in Piedmont a tiny kitchen
was installed off her bedroom for the preparation of her
kosher meals.]*

It's summer here again today, and I do hope it
will last for awhile. Harriet just came in and announced that we are going driving out in the country this afternoon—instead of going shopping, for
which little change of plan I am most grateful. I de-

test shopping worse than anything I know in the whole wide world. I just remembered I never told you a word about Rouen and we had such a beautiful trip! It was Pentacost so the whole country was having a holiday. The hotel was crowded but we managed to get rooms. The country is crowded with tourists in Limousines. It was a new one on me to see so many limousines, instead of touring cars way out in the country. The English and French do such a lot of touring, and they have it down pat, too. They take their maid and chauffeur and the most remarkable thing is how few machines get out of order. I think it is a law here about keeping the car in order. Rouen has three big cathedrals, supposed to be the most wonderful Gothic architecture in the world. They are magnificent, but somehow I like the cathedral in Chartres better. It is a little old town and is full of crooked streets, so very narrow. One interesting thing we saw is a ferry that goes across the river by pulley. It is way above the river, carries about a hundred people and just goes flying across. We took a little trip up the river, and asked the man on the boat what time he went back from the little village where we landed, he said right away but we could get another boat in about twenty-five minutes, so we started up the road gaily. We hadn't gone very far when it commences to rain, and we heard the boat whistle at the same time. Well, we ran for all we were worth, yelling to the little boat, which waited for us, and then took us back to Rouen. Outside of freezing to death, the river trip was most enjoyable.

Just came back from a perfectly wonderful afternoon in the country—the woods are marvellous! I only want to add that we stayed in Rouen two days and that I have ten minutes to get to the Post office which is six blocks away.

Loads of love,

Sis

May 20, 1913.

Dear Family:

We just came home from downtown, after having ordered a coat for me—I didn't take the last one. But what do you think? We got to the tailors at nine twenty and nobody was there yet—they say the French women do their shopping at eleven—never before. Anyhow, I am so relieved at really having found something that I can hardly believe its true. I never had such a job in all my life—have been just about everywhere in Paris except to a tailor where I should have gone first. Anyhow—that's over.

I am awful sleepy cause I have been up so many nights lately. Last night Mr. & Mrs. Cooper were in to dinner—seven o'clock dinner which was served at eight cause our guests did not arrive. Mr. Cooper is from S.F. and is here studying with Bauer, and teaching. He is immensely interesting and Harriet and he had a grand time diving into the whys and wherefores of various musical compositions. He is very young and will undoubtedly make good. After dinner Mr. Harden came in, he is a young man from Boston—loads of fun and just the easy-going kind. He sails for home next week, sad to say. When he came last night he announced that he had never seen a Matisse, so of course we all bundled him over to Steins. When we got there, we found a whole big bunch of Stein relatives from Baltimore who have just arrived on the scene of action. There is a Dr. Cone—a lady—who is a practicing physician in Baltimore and who has some kind of a chair at John Hopkins. Her sister, who is sick and has her trained nurse along. *[Dr. Clarabel and Miss Etta Cone were later to provide the Baltimore Museum of Art with a magnificent bequest, including hundreds of items by Matisse and substantial works of Courbet, Cézanne, Gauguin, and Picasso, among many other twentieth-century masters. Sylvia is wrong, however—they were not relatives of the Steins. Gertrude had met them when she was a medical student in Baltimore, where she and Miss Etta formed a particularly strong friendship.]* Dr. Cone is a picnic—so entertaining—she entertained the whole bunch last night with stories of customs—its all very funny while you sit over here perfectly comfortable, but I am sure that everything she said will pop into my head when I land at New York. One thing she said perfectly seriously, not knowing it was funny, was that the custom officers are always so nice—when they throw your Paris gowns down on the wharf they always apologize!

Yesterday afternoon I went bumming with two of the girls. We went to the awful Gallery Lafayette and looked for cheap little dresses for the country, and then, after having tried on every three and four dollar dress in the place, we went to tea at the swellest place in Paris. It is called Ciro's and they serve anything in the way of tea or coffee or ices and charge three francs per person—but the difference is that you can eat as much as you want, and everything is included in the three francs. We had cakes, sandwiches, tarts, eclaires, fruit tarts, and I can't remember what else. But they are all the very best I ever tasted any where. Every time you look up another boy comes running over with something else wonderful in the way of eats.

Our plans for the summer have undergone a complete change again—We are going to Aguay, a little place on the Mediterranean, not far from Monte Carlo, etc. with the Steins. *[Baedeker refers to Agay (as it is properly spelled) as "a little village in a charming setting on a bay." Its red porphyry rocks and cliffs are notable; it is on the Corniche d'or road, almost halfway between Nice and Marseille.]* They leave the first of July, to stay two months. Well, I thought I would go with them for a little while and then go to Switzerland where the Strausses are going—on Lake Geneva. It sounds good, doesn't it? I saw the pictures of Aguay last night, and they are beautiful, something like Carmel, only Carmel hasn't the blueness and calmness of the sea, and also hasn't the famous red rock.

I went to a concert the other night, given by a Mrs. McGee, I think—she used to sing in the Schul in S.F. She hasn't the voice that we all thought she had, but it may have been because she hasn't been well. There are so many people over here who tell you what handsome voices they have, but when it comes to hearing them sing it is a bit different. But there was a little Spanish girl age fifteen, who played the piano. I haven't heard anything so exquisite and finished since I have been here. She is marvellous—pretty as a picture and with perfect poise. She played something of her own for an encore, and it was delightful—everyone is so enthusiastic about her here.

Sunday afternoon one of the girls and I went over to the Bois. I had a fight with the driver of our cab and when he stood up and screamed a volley of

French at me I wanted to laugh. The Bois is always so crowded and of course the French love excitement, so I furnished them a nice little entertainment. It was so funny! We went to a tea place in the Bois which is patronized by the Chic people—not the demi-monde. There was such a mob there that we really only got a kind of bird's eye view of the chics, but it was a lot of fun.

I think I am a bit written out, but I just must tell you about an evening I went to last week, where somebody played the most wonderful rag ever, and where I discovered I haven't out-grown it in the least—I thought I had, but all I needed was to hear some of the old things well played. Everybody was absolutely aus-gelassen. I haven't laughed so hard in months and years—two of the boys dressed up in feather dusters and rugs and things, anything they could lay their hands on—and the make-ups were clever as they could be. We made so much noise that the concierge came up and asked us to please close the windows—and we heard next day that everyone in the house was at their windows listening.

Lots of love to everybody,

Sis

May 27, 1913

Dear Family:

Harriet has gone over to Steins for a nap cause the painters are painting the windows here—they are all over the place, and our maid is having the time of her life. Yesterday afternoon when I came home, I walked in and this was the picture I saw—the two men, one at either side of the room, standing perfectly transfixed, and Marie in the middle with my new spring bonnet on. It was so cute, and they were all having such a good time all I could do was make believe I hadn't seen it. She complains all the time of how the men mess up the house, etc.—and she is in seventh heaven having them here. The Blumingdales are coming in to tea this afternoon—Harriet and I met Josie Blumingdale on the street the other day—first time I have run into anyone I knew—she came flying after us yelling "Harriet."

And it is hot! We are having the most marvellous summer weather you could imagine. Everyone is complaining of the heat, and I adore it. This morning I was able for the first time since I have been here, to wash my own hair. It was so good to be able to do it and then stick your head out the window and dry it in the sun! You can't imagine how good it felt—it dried in fifteen minutes!

I went to one of the big markets—one of the swell ones, this morning, and saw all the wonderful fruits and things. They have our delicatessen shops beaten to a frazzle when it comes to dainties in the way of salads and things. I punished myself by making myself watch an eel—it is considered a great delicacy—but, not for me. They have the eels and fishes and lobsters, crabs etc. all alive, and it gives me the jimjams—especially the eels. But I can't stand it when I am standing looking at the shellfish and it begins to move.

Last night we went to the Russian Ballet. They did Sheherazade (I had to get the programme to find out how to spell it.) The man, Adolphe Bolm, is supposed to be a wonder, but I don't think any of them are in the same class with Pavlova and Mordkin. *[Adolphe Bolm was Diaghilev's premier danseur; Mikhail Mordkin was Pavlova's partner—Sylvia must have seen Mordkin on his and Pavlova's triumphal 1910 tour of the United States.]* The woman Mme. Karsavina, also supposed to be a wonder, was not too good. The man really did it remarkably well! But it was frightful. The sliminess of it—The men were all negroes—I think it was about the most horrible thing I have ever seen. The second thing was a little creation called "Jeux." The music was Debussy and it was extraordinary—the whole thing so different from anything I have ever seen, and very well done. The "Spectre of the rose" was so pretty and dainty—a very cute idea and well done in spots. It is supposed to be one of their finest. Then the last thing was Polish Dancers. It was all one grand rough-house, no speed limit and never a slow-down for one second. The stage looked quite mad—but it was all wonderful. *[Sergei Diaghilev brought his troupe from Russia to Paris for the first time in 1909;* Scheherazade *and* The Specter of the Rose *both date from 1911.* Jeux, *Diaghilev's first ballet in modern dress, received its world premier during this 1913 season; it was danced by Mme. Karsavina and its choreographer, Waslaw Nijinsky.]* The most exciting part of the evening, per usual, was the audience. It was a beautiful house—always packed, but not always beautifully gowned. While we were promenading between numbers, in the good old way, we saw a woman who was so beautiful that everyone just formed a kind of circle around her and stared. She had brilliant red hair, with green combs in it, and a green fantasie that went like a peacock's tail on the front of her hair. Her gown was white, perfectly simple beaded cloth—her figure was marvellous and she walked like a queen. She was the attraction of the place, even though there were a great many wonders. Harriet asked one of the ushers who she was and he said she comes all the time—nobody knows her, she always has wonderful make-ups and jewels, and, he told Harriet very confidentially she never gives anybody a sou. It was awfully funny. Harriet bought a new thing for her hair, and you should have seen Marie when she saw Harriet with something in her hair and me without anything. Marie is my old stand-by—she thinks I am wonderful, but she can't bear seeing anyone with any thing better than I have.

Sunday afternoon we had a wonderful time! A whole crowd of us went up the river to Longchamps, to see the polo-meet, which, by the way didn't come off. Mr. Norledge took us and he is dandy to go places with. I saw so many things I had never seen before—a hydroplane on the river, and eleven baloons racing—the hydroplane wasn't racing—don't misunderstand me—But it was great seeing all those big baloons racing across the sky, each with one man in the basket. Then we passed a most peculiar game—I don't know the name of it, but there is one man in each boat, and he stands on a kind of platform in the front of the boat, and has a long pole with which he gives his opponent a poke, and tries to knock him into the river—lots of fun! Well, even though they were not playing polo, we managed to see a couple of perfectly good horse-races. Then we had an ice at one of the big cafés, sitting out under the trees. Then we walked around through the bois to a place called Passy, where we took a taxi home. It was some fine afternoon. The girls were dead tired—because you see,

Mr. Norledge and I set the pace, not realizing we were walking so far. But I guess they have recovered by now.

Loads of love,

Sis

Dear Family:

A letter from Mrs. Peabody arrived t'other day. It was such fun—we screamed at it. It was so wonderfully as if Grandma had written it.

It is still staying hot here, so I just kind of run around half-dressed all day, and love it. We had a wonderful time yesterday afternoon—we took the six o'clock boat down the river, about an hour's run—a whole bunch of us—and took supper along, and sat out under the trees on the shore of the river and ate. It was so beautiful and we just giggled and had a dandy time. After we finished our supper we went to one of the cafés out there and sat outside and had lemonade. We got home at about half past ten. Going down on the boat there was an old man sitting next to me, and in trying to make room for one of our bunch I bumped into him, thus causing him to move a bit, after which I thanked him, in French, and we all proceeded to laugh and talk about him. Well, after a little while, he said to me, in perfectly good American, "You're American, aren't you?" Can you imagine me? I almost expired! But he turned out to be a very nice man who is travelling alone, and who is exceedingly lonely because all his children, six, are married, etc. We dis-

cussed the Japanese situation in America and aeroplanes, steamers and languages, and then he got
off. Poor old man, I did my hardest to cheer him up
a bit. But it was a dandy picnic!

Harriet informed me a while ago that she is
going to the country about a half hour from Paris,
to stay for a couple of days. It is the place the Norledges go to all the time, and is very lovely. So,
Theresa is coming to stay with me. Harriet is going
tomorrow morning, Saturday, and will probably be
back Monday. *[Harriet spent the three days in
Barbizon.]*

We are going to tea with the Baltimore people
this afternoon. I hope they have sense enough to
take us to some place where we can eat out under
the trees. Josie Blumingdale and her sister Bertha
were in to tea. Josie is a picnic! Every thing she says
is funny. She has been over here for six years and
hasn't any intention of going home at all. The two
of them just keep travelling, some times together,
and some times not.

I have to go for a lesson now, so—My French
teacher has been sick so I've had a vacation for
a week.

Loads of love,

Sis

June 6, 1913

Dear Family:

Yesterday morning I was sitting all curled up in
my dressing gown when Albert walked in. He looks
fine, has a mustache again, and is fat, a little too

fat, I think. He has been working very hard in Vienna and is here now, looking for a studio in which he can make about six or eight hours noise a day. Yesterday after lunch I went round to Steins to ask about a place for Albert, we met Matisse there. I thought it was rather funny that Albert was so indifferent in his presence, but decided it was because every one was talking French, and Albert doesn't understand very well. When Matisse left, and I happened to mention something about him, Albert almost killed me, he was so mad at me for not having told him who he was. It is the first time I have met Matisse—it would have been most pleasant for me if I hadn't had heart failure in the excitement and been afraid to talk. It was just the same thing the other night when I met such a nice French fellow who is master of philosophy etc. and whom the hostess of the evening plunked down next to me on the couch. I had to talk, but it took me almost fifteen minutes to recover my equilibrium enough to make real conversation.

Oh, yes, I wanted to tell you about the fun we had while Harriet was away. Theresa stayed with me, but about all she did was to sleep here for two nights—we were out all the time. Sunday night I had six young people in to supper—a regular old Salinger Sunday evening supper. It was lots of fun— the maid was out, so every body piled in and helped. After supper some more people came in and in the midst of it all Sally's maid came flying in to tell her the baby was crying, so we all took the party and went over there. It was all one grand rough-house, and my party was considered a great success.

T'other night we went to see Boris Godonow, the big Russian Opera. It is not what it is cracked up to be—most of us thought, but we enjoyed it just the same. *[Boris Godunov had had its first Paris performance in 1908.]* The color was beautiful—the music very nice in parts, etc. We have sold our ballet seats, cause we thought once was enough, and anyhow, if it had been Pavlova and Mordkin it might have been an other story.

I had to stop for a minute to go to the bakers, and insulted the girl by asking her why she always had the same kind of cake so one never could have a change. Anyhow, I managed to come out all right. Went down town this morning and in passing the dog store, I saw a wolf-hound for sale. Went in and asked the price—$120 and he is seventeen months. It was too cheap so I didn't buy him.

Again, I was interrupted—I've been with Albert to the apartment which he has taken—and, acting as interpreter is no joke. I am a wreck.

Loads of love,

SIS

June 12, 1913

Dear Family:

Harriet says to tell you she would like to write but can't because she strained her eyes and is resting them for a while. We are so dreadfully busy trying to get ready to go away at the end of next week, that we really haven't time for any thing else these days. We leave a week from Saturday, June 21, a little more than a week before we expected. We are all going down to Agay together, the Steins, Theresa, Miss Miller, Harriet and me. They say it is dreadfully hot, so we are getting a few little

nothings to wear there—meaning, a few little thin-
nesses—very few, I assure you.

I got a dandy big letter from Ruth! Its fine for
her to have the house in Piedmont. *[Ruth Elkus and
her children spent the summer in a rented house in Piedmont; this seems to have had no connection with the
house to which all the other Salingers eventually moved.]*
I was so glad to hear about that. By the way, are
they having the swimming course at U.C. again this
summer? Should love to know—am that curious!

Better begin now to address letters to the bank,
we stand a better chance of getting them than when
re-addressed to the apartment.

Loads of love to everybody,

Sis

*[The following letter was begun by Harriet and com-
pleted by Sylvia.]*

[undated]

Dear Family—

I strained my eyes a short time ago and am not
using them more than I can help—so please excuse
me from writing for a little while longer.

We are leaving Saturday the 21st for Agay—
and are about ready—bathing suits—water wings
and all.

I'll only go into the water to get wet as I believe
myself past the desire for youthful athletics. But I
have a gorgeous cap—orange with a black bow.

It has been very hot this last week but I do not
seem to mind it. Wait a minute—here are Sis and

Albert and I'll let Sis finish the letter. *[And Sylvia takes over.]*

She does that very same thing all the time—puts up a big bluff at writing a letter—and then leaves me to finish. We are in the midst of all kinds of excitement now, trying to get things cleared up to go away on the coming Saturday. I have been chasing around trying to rent some sheets for Albert, he sets up house-keeping tomorrow in the pretty little atelier.

It is very warm—but I really like it so much—so long as I don't have to run around too much. Last night we had a crowd of about ten in, and instead of giving them tea, I fixed lemonade with ice in it, and it was muchly appreciated. We had such a lovely simple evening—every one enjoyed it so much. They all begged me to sing, and I was getting more scared every minute until I suddenly remembered that all my music was at Strausses house. It was a relief. I don't know why I get so scared at the thought of singing for any one but I imagine it is because I am not yet quite sure of my pitch, even though it has improved marvellously! Yesterday morning I had one of the best lessons I have ever had. We were both so pleased—then, at the end of the lesson, Albert came in and they insisted upon my singing for him. I sang three songs and at the end of the third my throat was so parched from sheer fright that I could hardly talk. Albert seemed to think my voice was nice, but of course, it is hard to tell under those circumstances. I am concentrating on pitch now, so that I can feel more sure—I never would have believed that anyone could improve so greatly in such a short time.

Yesterday afternoon I went to an exhibition of a collection to be sold today. It is the most wonderful collection I have seen—from the old Grecos down to all the modern men. The things are glorious— There was one little Corot that I wanted to put in a bid for, but was afraid some one else would bid higher—there were too many limousines around. I don't see how in the world one man can own so many wonderful old and new things.

Saturday night was the Steins last At Home of the season, so we made it a gala by dressing up. There was a perfect mob there—a lot of us in evening dress, and it was one of the nicest evenings they have had. The Arnstein girls from S.F. were there—they left on Sunday for home via London. They are very nice girls, but staid such a short time in Paris. *[One Arnstein girl, Mabel, was later to marry Sylvia's brother Jeffrey.]*

There are some people outside making such a racket slamming tin roofs around that I find it very difficult to think.

Lots of love to everybody,

Sis

[Sylvia's first letter from the Riviera follows.]

June 24, 1913

Dear Family:

I guess you think that by this time I am lost or strayed or stolen—but I forgot to figure on more time for my letter to get to a boat to be taken across the ocean.

This is the most gloriously wonderful place I have ever been in in my entire existence—the crowd, Steins, Theresa, Rachel Miller, Harriet and I just hit it off right. One couldn't wish for a more perfect situation—every body does just about what every body else wants them to do, so that sort of thing always leads to contentment.

The Mediterranean is blue—just like it tells about it in all the books—we go in swimming every morning about ten, and spend the rest of the time up till lunch swimming and drying in the sun. I have arms that are as red as coals, and I tried awful hard to be careful. The water is the kind that is so salty it just holds you up whether you want to stay up or not. You can float for hours, I am sure. The whole place is wonderfully like Carmel, only so much nicer. The food is wonderful—everything so well cooked—and all fresh—vegetables, fruit of all sorts—such peaches—fish—everything raised right here. I am going to let Harriet explain all that because she can do it better than I, all about the food, and how cheap it is, 7 francs a day, etc.

The trip down was delightful—we felt like regular Cook's tours—Mr. Stein kept the tickets, reserved the rooms at Marseilles, where we stayed over night—did all the tipping—just every thing—that's what I call travelling! And he is so nice to everybody that they do any thing for him. Even the conductor on the train helped with the luggage when we changed at San Rafael. We got in to Marseilles too late to see anything there, so we are going to stop over on our way back, for a couple of days.

The climate is perfect—just warm enough, and not too warm! The rocks are all kinds of red and beautiful, and most important of all, we eat on the veranda overlooking the Sea. You see, we are not on the sea proper, but on what is called Agay bay. It is a little bay, with beautiful curves, and a lovely beach, and the advantage is that it never gets rough. But, I can sit on my little balcony and watch the ships on the sea, so you can get an idea of how little the bay is. When we take walks in the woods we get the most delicious odors imaginable—all kinds of wonderful smelly flowers and pine trees and things. And, yesterday I heard my first nightingale—the woods are full of them, and how they sing! I don't remember of ever having had such a feeling of perfect calm, as you get here—there isn't one thing to complain of, not one. We have a little store just across the road, where we can buy all the regular country things, the maids are all pretty and sweet—everything is spick span clean, and all the washing is done by the Italian women, in a river about a block from the hotel. I am trying to tell you all the details, but they seem to be slipping away.

There is a big hotel up on the hill a little way off which is supposed to be terrible swell, but which is closed for the summer. They have some tennis courts over there which we had hoped to be able to use, but upon investigating, found them to be decidedly overgrown with weeds.

We go to bed early and get up early, which life always appealed to me. The people are mostly transients, who tour in big limousines, but there are a few who are very nice looking though we never say more than good morning and good evening to them. A German couple and a French couple, and a French family of mother, father and young son etc.

Now I can't think of any more, but just want to ask you please not to expect too much in the way of letters, because you know the sameness of summer resort life, and, after all, there isn't much to write.

The Strausses stayed in Paris on account of being more comfortable with the baby there, so my voice is getting a rest.

Loads of love, and please write lots all the time.

Sis

[The following is a postcard from Agay.]

June 27, 1913

Dear Family:

It is impossible to figure on boats from here, so I'll write every so often and take a chance. Just came in from a most handsome swim! Have rented a <u>bicycle</u> by the month, and Mr. Stein and I just go riding all over the country, its great!!

Lots of love,

Sis.

June 29, 1913

Dear Family:

We go swimming every morning and jump rope and do exercises and things in the sun afterward—so, our mornings are always the same. The eventful times are the afternoons. I forgot to say, I usually practice in the mornings before the swim.

Yesterday, for lunch, they gave us the wonderful treat of the dish of the country. It is rare, and so the lady of the house stood at the door watching how we would take it. Well, it came on the table in a big dish, that is about the size of three ordinary soup bowls. It contained whole fish and whole lobsters—little ones. It looked exactly like the bottom of the Sea let loose on the table. Mr. Stein served, and no one said a word. I was so speechless that he had to ask me three times for my plate before I heard him. When my plate came back to me with one whole lobster and one whole fish—it was altogether too realistic—I couldn't do the work, try as I did. Finally, I looked up, and found Harriet's eyes glued on me—Well, I went into hysterics, and waited for the meat course. You should have seen the look of relief on Rachel's face when I told her under the table that I couldn't consider it for a minute. Harriet said she tried four times to keep herself at the table and finally succeeded in so doing. Theresa and the Steins adored it, and we decided that the next time we shall go to the next village for lunch, while those who like it can have the treat. I have never experienced such a peculiar under-the sea sensation. It was frightful!

In the afternoon we all went over to Trayas, which is supposed to be the show place of the Mediterranean. It is about two hours driving over the most beautiful road imaginable—right along the coast, over the hills, with the blue sea and red rock always in front or at the side. The ladies drove in the carriage and we rode our bicycles. It was glorious. We had tea and lemonade and things on the veranda at Trayas and then came home just about in time for dinner. It is supposed to be the only place where you find the wonderful redness of the rock, and, in contrast to the blueness of the sea, it is wonderful. It is just right as to warmth—not too hot for riding in the sun, and not too cool in the shade without wraps. The evenings are perfect—

without any wrap one is most comfortable, mostly always.

I am balancing the tablet on one knee—that's why it is so kind of scribbly.

Lots of love,

Sis

[A letter from Harriet follows.]

Grand Hotel, Agay-Var., France, June 30

Dear Family:

It's an ideal place that we have found—a place well frequented in the winter by Strangers—and during the summer by the French.

Our little hotel is right over a pretty bay—sheltered and cooled by the sea breeze.

The weather has been perfect. In Paris they are wearing straw hats and overcoats—Here we are in linens and sandals—and are perfectly comfortable.

We eat on a broad porch overlooking the water and the meals are fine, homelike and excellently prepared.

They tried the special dish of the country on us the other day—boullabase it is called. I had heard of it but was not prepared for it. Two big dishes were brought in—one containing lobsters and a queer finny black fish—all whole. Another great bowl held slices of toasted bread lost in a saffron sauce. I felt as if I was having a bad nightmare in which I was lost in an acquarium. I tried to eat some of it—and it took me 24 hours to believe that the world was not a saturation of saffron. Mike &

Sarah & Theresa pronounced it fine and ate up the whole dish.

I have been in bathing twice—and expect to learn to swim—and after swimming we lie in the sun to dry.

Everybody here thinks that Theresa and Sylvia belong to Sarah—they both look very young in their summer clothes and not unlike Sarah. Sylvia has rented a wheel [*a bicycle*] and is seeing the country & trying the ice cream of all the adjacent towns.

Much love to all from

HARRIET

Agay, France, July 15, '13

Dear Family:

I was afraid when we first came down that I wouldn't have anything to write, and now, we have been doing so much that I hardly know where to begin.

We go in swimming twice a day now, having discovered that the water is so cool after a dusty walk in the afternoon—and we find it just as pleasurable and much more fun to swim than to wash for dinner. I consider that quite an important item.

Yesterday was the fourteenth, and therefore a big day for France. There were loads of people here to dinner—people touring in all kinds of things, limousines, touring cars, motor-cycles, bicycles, everything that ever was. Wouldn't have been a bit surprised to have seen an air-ship drop in. In the evening the whole country around was sending off fire-works. They shot the sky-rockets out over the bay, and with the wonderful moonlight, it was a beautiful sight. Then the people in the villa next door had a lot of that red, green, and white fire stuff. It was all very handsome, but we sort of felt it was ten days late.

We took a climb yesterday up to the top of some where or other, and had the most beautiful view of all sides of the country. We could see all the way over to Cannes and beyond—to the Alps with their snow-capped tops—at the same time, we had the view of the biggest expanse of sea I have ever seen. It looked so blue, and the sail boats looked so pretty on it.

Rachael had a birthday the other day, and we went to Cannes to celebrate. We just kind of bought out the town, including two dishes of ice-cream a piece (great luxury) and then came home in time for our swim. We had a birthday cake at dinner, and they wanted to fix it, so I suggested sticking the candles in it as we always do at home when we haven't holders, which we were unable to get. You should have heard the howl that went up—the cake had been specially ordered at San Rafael, Mr. Stein had to go down for it, on his bicycle—so they re-fused to let me stick my candles in, instead of which, they stuck them on a piece of card board and laid it on top of the cake. It was most success-ful—when the cake was cut, the card-board was simply taken off, and the candles burned down. We had some joshes for Rachael, and it being all a great surprise to her, we had a lot of fun.

Oh! my, you should have seen the picnic we had tother day. It was hot as anything, and we walked along at a great rate. Rachael wasn't very well, so we all kind of helped her along. We had a wonderful lunch put up by the lady of the hotel here. Each one had a sandwich—which was a half-loaf of bread with ham, and meat in it, and then covered by the other half of the loaf. No-one was at all particular about showing the size of their mouths, but just went right to it. Then we had more bread, with cheese, and an enormous box of fruit—peaches, figs, apricots, plums, and I don't know what else. Everybody was comfortably lying around when Mr. Stein decided we should walk home by way of Trayas, which meant a tremendous (for the others) climb over a big grade. Well, Allan got behind Harriet, and I got behind Rachael, and we pushed them, leaving the rest to hobble along. We made it all right, went to Trayas for drinks, took the train home from there, and those who still had some surplus energy went for a swim. It was a splendid day, and everybody did good work.

Yesterday a big box of candy and glaced fruits arrived from Nice from some friends of the Steins who spent the day with us one day last week. They came in the morning, had lunch, and tea, watched us swim, had a walk, I mean a ramble, and stayed to dinner, and left in the eight train for Nice. They had just come from Spain and gave us wonderful descriptions of dirty hotels, frightfully hot weather, horrible bull-fights, etc.—so Harriet and I decided we were kind of glad we hadn't gone.

I guess the only thing left is a walk we took with our French friends before they left. We climbed up a mountain in search of a view, as usual. The going up was all right, but you should have seen the coming down. We lost our way, and had to fight through the brush—It was all right for the men and me, but the ladies—Harriet and Madame French—had an awful time. Finally we came to a path—all rocks and nice slippery pine needles—they slid and screamed the whole way down—I only wished I had had my Kodak, but I didn't. In the middle of the descent, the Madame stopped short and said she couldn't do it, she was going back—I don't know where she expected to go when she went back— we hadn't any idea how we got to where we were. But we persuaded her and—got home just in time to slap some water on my face and change my dress for dinner.

Harriet always comes home so fresh, and not the least bit tired, from our walks. Isn't it splendid?

Lots of love to everybody,

Sis

[The following letter is from Harriet.]

Agay-Var. France, July 20, 1913

Dear Jeffrey:

I want to write about the sale of the house. I see the question differently these days. Now, it seems to me far fetched to displace a whole family because of one. As I remember, your father wants to remain there because he likes it. Your mother wants to remain because she dreads the effort of change. The reasons for moving outside of Sylvia's question are the depreciation in the property values—and the esthetic (?) undesirability of the location. Your father is indifferent about the depreciation in value—it isn't important.

The change in neighborhood—as far as it will affect the happiness of the family—I believe to be equally unimportant. Anybody may get married or leave Oakland—or make any change at any time—within the next five years. And the expense will be enormous—a great strain on your father—and almost unnecessary.

So, I cannot but feel it is a little mad to make the change because of one girl's ridiculous love affair.

I shouldn't do it, if I were any of you. Either she could stay over here until the schoolhouse is built—or she could go home—and live in the house. Let me know please right away—when the schoolhouse is to be finished or when it is to be begun and finished. *[Harriet's cryptic references to "the schoolhouse" presumably concern Sylvia's plan to become a teacher of the Montessori method.]*

At present I should pronounce Sylvia cured completely—not at any high moral strain at all—at all. She speaks of her Oakland friend to the other girls with an ease that leaves me a little breathless. *[It seems quite possible that by this time the dogged devotion of Allan Stein had assuaged Sylvia's grief over her forced separation from the Coffee boy. In Salinger family discussions, by the way, Sylvia's lover was never referred to in any other way—it was always "the Coffee boy" sans given name—nor was what happened to him ever revealed.]*

If she were living next door—and got lonely for some one to make love to her—she might of course drift back—I can guarantee nothing for my sex. But present indications are against that. However, as she has come over to get free from her love affair—and as she has achieved it, it would seem nice, if possible, to postpone her coming home until the school house was completed, or the boy has had time to recover—or go away—or do something convenient. We are wondering, by the way, why Charlie has not written telling of his interview with him. *[There is no record of this interview between Sylvia's lawyer brother-in-law and the boy who just wasn't good enough for Sylvia's mother.]* It might give us some lead as to his future attitude. That would be helpful. But not under any circumstances would I move away because of the boy.

I'll write to you as soon as I have anything to offer. In the meantime, you have all the love of

Your fond

HARRIET

Agay, July 24, '13

Dear Family:

Agay is always the same delightful place week in and week out. The time is just running away from us here, and I do so hate to think of leaving.

We went down to San Rafael on our bicycles the other day and saw a whole fleet of battleships coming into the harbor—they looked like destroyers, only larger. After they anchored, we could see the men diving into the water and swimming around. There were a lot of people along the shore, it being the regular French vacation time, and it really was a pretty sight.

We had a few weeds taken out of the tennis court, and go over there and fool around every once in a while. We can't really play, mostly because Allan is the only one who knows how, and then, because the court isn't good enough. It is funny about tennis—how you get all out of practice and it is just as if you had never played at all. Rachael used to play well, and now she is learning just the same as Theresa who never played at all.

Yesterday when we went in swimming, there were real waves and it is such fun to float on them—it is just like being in a cradle—and this water is so buoyant, its wonderful.

Can't think of anything exciting to write about so guess I'll stop.

Lots of love,

Sis

Agay, July 30, '13

Dear Family:

The most exciting thing that Agay has to boast of of late is—Mrs. Stein's birthday. We all got up early in the morning and bounced in on her, each with a little gift, before she was half awake. It was such fun, and she loved it all. Theresa and Mr. Stein had gone to Cannes a few days before to buy the things, and we managed to get quite a collection of things she likes. In the afternoon we celebrated by driving over a road over which they had not yet been—along the Sea, and then way up in the mountains. Mr. Stein, Allan and I on our bicycles, and the rest driving. We missed connections, and had to wait about two hours for them in San Rafael, but we waited at a very nice café so it was all right. And, I had the extreme pleasure of seeing the most beautiful double-overhand stroke I have ever seen. The man went along as if he were wound up, in perfect rhythm, and slowly and most perfectly. It was a joy to watch him. Speaking of

swimming, Harriet is slowly but surely learning. It won't be long before she swims. The great difficulty is that each time I let her go a little bit she decides it is time to get up on her feet. It is most disconcerting. But now back to the birthday. We got home before the carriage people, and, even though we were late for dinner, we flew down for a dip.
We got home at a quarter to seven, and when we came back from our plunge it was five minutes past. Pretty good, no? And, we were all ready by the time the rest arrived. When we went down to dinner we found the maids had decorated the table— so prettily. Wasn't it nice of them? We had ice-cream, special home-made coffee ice-cream that was too good for words. The man who runs the place is a wonder chef, and he himself made the cream for us. Then, with the black coffee, the maid brought on the tray with candles all lighted, and you should have seen Mrs. Stein—she looked like a scared child. After which we had joshes, with verses, all on her. Altogether it was a most joyous occasion— and we all thanked her for having a birthday.

The other night, an automobile party dropped in to dinner, and when I heard one man say to the other, "They do it in all the garages so I don't see why we can't," I lost my head completely and nothing could move me from the spot. I would never have believed it if anyone told me that the American language could have such a fascination for me. I just kind of stood around and listened to them talk—They were so American! There were about seven men and two women, in a couple of touring cars. It was a treat!

Loads of love to everybody,

Sis

Dear Family:

We have discovered something new about making our bathing comfortable. I have a big heavy bath robe which I put over me, after taking off my wet suit, and sit in the sun. It feels so good, all the difference in the world, then we don't have to bring our wet suits up into our rooms at all. We just take them off down at the bath house and hang them on the line.

Yesterday was a fete day at San Rafael so we went down on our bicycles, at the same time seeing some people off who had made the tour from Geneva on bicycles. She is a very nice little woman and she spoke such a nice French that we got along beautifully.

The whole country was there all down on the shore watching the game they play here. It is most peculiar—A big row boat, six men rowing, and at the end of the boat a kind of thing built like this *[Sylvia here draws an object that looks very much like an oriental soup spoon, with a tiny man standing on the tip of the handle.]* with the man standing up at the top with a long pole. Well, they row like mad (two boats), passing each other so close they touch, while the men on the platform poke at each other to see which can knock the other into the water. The first time they both fell in, and when they came up they swam to each other and kissed. It was so funny! The second two—one lost his pole—etc. It is not very exciting because it takes so long for them to row way off and all the way back each time. It was interesting, though, to see the crowd, the boats little and big going in and out, until there were so many little boats around that you could have walked from one to the other—they were just kind of stacked up. In the midst of it all, my keen eye discovered a little canoe, three men paddling, and at one end a perfectly good American flag. I almost lost my head completely.

Well, we stayed there a while, then took our friends to tea, and then they left us.

Lots of love to everyone,

Sis

Agay, France, August 10, '13

Dearest Ruthie:

We are going to stay on here till after my birthday, then on to Paris. Are you surprised that we are coming home? I am so happy to think I can, and to think that I really feel that I have gained enough common sense over here to help out at 911 a bit.

Did you know the Strauss family were sailing in Sept.? Sally will probably look you up to get some notes on Babies. But isn't it wonderful for me to have Laurie there? He is a really exceptional teacher—everyone who has come in contact with him says the same thing and all the biggest men in Paris praise his voice to the skies. I am quite sure he will startle San Francisco when they hear how very much he really has to offer. I won't be able to sing when I get home until after I take a few lessons.

We are going to Nice for a couple of days this week, I think. It is about a two hours train trip, and I think it worthwhile to take a look at Nice and Monte Carlo so long as we are so close.

I suppose you know that we are staying here

until about the middle of September. Think of it!—
almost three whole months in the country—with
swimming in the blue Mediterranean twice a day.
The blumin' old blue Mediterranean has suddenly
turned cold, however, so there isn't much chance
for any fancy stunts, just good hard swimming
to keep from congealing. The wind from Africa
brought the cold water in the other day, but they
tell us here it will warm up again, so long as the
wind stays in Africa!

Jimmy wrote that Papa is considering a run-a-
bout (for me to drive?) and just while I was tip-top
in my excitement Harriet announced that she didn't
believe it. I won't down my hopes, anyhow. *[Among
her many accomplishments, Sylvia was most proud of her
ability to drive the family motor car. For years she was
their chauffeur, since her father, mother, and aunt Lena
Sickles never did learn to drive.]*

Lots of love to you and your family,

Sis

Agay, France, Aug. 15, '13

Dear Family:

I am in the arbor here, trying to write, with the
paper flying all over the universe. The wind is blow-
ing at the rate of seventeen hundred miles an hour.

Let me tell you what I did yesterday. I discovered where a filling had come out of my tooth. So,
Mr. Stein and I went to Cannes to a very good den-
tist. He said there was nothing—my mouth was in
perfect condition. I felt like a fool—But I had the
consolation of knowing he didn't know I had come
all the way from Agay. It is about forty minutes by
train.

So, we did some shopping, consisting mostly of candy, and had tea at the café on the shore of the sea, then walked out on the pier where all the big millionaire yachts are—and had a grand time. Gordon Bennett's yacht—the biggest one around here—was open, the men working on it—the gang plank already there for me to walk right in. It was all I could do to stay off. It is a young ocean liner—I have never seen anything so big since I left the "Amerika" and to think it all belongs to one man. After inspecting the yachts, we went all around the old town. It looks like a typical Italian village, Mr. Stein says. Most of the people are Italian and it is really very interesting—it is all so old. The civilized end of Cannes, which has only been in existence about fifty years, looks like New York, next to the old end.

Harriet wishes me to state that she can float on her back all alone—and that I said she had the wierdest foot motion I had ever seen. I almost had hysterics this morning when I was trying to find out what was wrong with her foot strokes. She does such funny things—but she swims on her back most beautifully, really—so I think in another week, she'll be swimming on her front.

Lots of love to everybody,

Sis

Agay, August 20, '13

Dear Family:

Just stopped to take a swim and now I am dressed a bit ahead of time so shall finish this before lunch! Harriet distinguished herself this morning by really swimming alone. She started by herself, swam about six strokes toward me, and got up before she reached me. She will be swimming alone in all confidence before long, I am sure.

I am still trying to dive. I can do it from the springboard now, but not standing up, only kind of sitting on my heels and then going off. Still, I consider that I have made rather good progress when I consider how I tried to dive out at the pool last year and couldn't come any where near it. N'est-ce pas? Oui, c'est vrai.

There goes the bell for lunch.

J'ai bien mangé—and even after a tremendous lunch, we each had two big caramels out of Rachael's box which came from America day before yesterday. Rachael has a man. It makes it so pleasant for our "tummies."

Did you know Rachael is going to sail with us? But of course she only goes as far as New York. We had sent for passages, I mean, sailings, of the different steamers, but haven't decided yet which it will be. Harriet has such a strong dislike for the German, no one ever travels French, etc. So, I don't know yet, but it will be some time about the end of October, any how.

Don't let Babe forget to send me a list of the records you have at home. It will be most decidedly worth while for everybody.

Lots of love,

Sis

Agay, France, Aug. 27, 1913

Dear Family:

I do thank you, Lena, for your very sweet birthday wishes—even though they are just exactly a week ahead of time. I have to keep telling myself I am almost twenty-five. It doesn't seem possible that I am more than eighteen—doesn't feel like it, anyway.

There was a bit of excitement the other day when a handsome box of candy walked in from Maskey's. Mr. Max Rosenberg sent it to me. He was at the house in Paris when the box came from the boys to Harriet, and saw the joy it occasioned me. Wasn't it nice of him?

We are not staying here until the end of September, as we had planned, but are leaving on the second. Harriet and I are going to stay a couple of days in Marseille, to look around a bit, but Theresa and Rachael are going on to Paris. We thought we'd let Mrs. Stein and family finish up the last three weeks alone, so that she may be thoroughly rested before going back to her work in Paris. So, as soon as we get to Paris we are going to visit the various steamship companies and find out what is going on for October.

So far as Agay is concerned, it is the most wonderful spot on earth—without exception. I almost hate to leave—but I do want to get home! All we talk about now is swimming—Harriet and Rachael have both learned since they are here—and I am slowly but quite surely learning to dive. Yesterday I tried over and over, and flopped so many times that I am covered with black and blue spots, and can't laugh yet without my stomach hurting like anything. I am trying to <u>do</u> the dive I <u>taught</u> last summer at the pool.

It seems too bad to leave here on my birthday, but they have promised me my celebration at luncheon, instead of dinner, and, anyhow, the Strauss family sail on the seventh, and we want to see them—especially Theresa, wants to go up to Paris soon enough to have a few days with Sallie.

We didn't make the Nice trip after all, cause we found out that everything is closed there at this time of the year—And the only thing open at Monte Carlo is the gambling room, and that doesn't interest me in the least—and, it is much too hot for three hours in the train—to see nothing.

Last night a band of gypsies camped in the road, almost in front of our hotel. There were millions of them, it seemed—when, in reality, there were only two wagons full. They were all sizes and ages, and so dirty! The babies beg, and the older men steal, the women begging, too. When we started for our swim, we saw them all in our water, even to the horse and dog. It was awful—but we managed to find a clean part of the bay—and not to swallow too much water. After dinner the proprietor here told us not to leave anything out, so we proceeded to gather our bathing suits, which were out drying, and our bicycles, all into the house. It was funny to see the mad rush everybody made after their things. The gypsies slept in their wagons, and departed at seven o'clock this morning so all is once more calm and peaceful on the Mediterranean.

Loads of love to everybody,

Sis

[A letter from Harriet follows.]

August 30

Dear Jeffrey:

It is six thirty in the morning. There was some welcome rain in the night and the morning is lovely.

The weather and the water are so varied that there has been no monotony over these ten weeks. Of course it has been the swimming that has interested me most. I grew discouraged for a while—for after making a good beginning—I suddenly became fearful and seemed to go back. But last week, it came all at once—and now I am quite happy, swimming about 30 strokes—and floating on my back. When I return, I shall take the course at the Lurline Baths—as I think it the pleasantest recreation I know. I'll take your mother with me too. She would like it—and it takes all the kinks out.

We leave on the 2nd for Marseilles, where we remain a day—and then return to Paris. As soon as we get there we will arrange for steamer accomodations. The rates change on the fifteenth of October—that is, the minimum rate always remains the same, but we can secure good accomodations instead of the poor ones of the minimum price.

We shall go back to our apartment, as we have left our belongings there (we didn't pay during our absence) and it is cheaper and more comfortable than the only little hotel in the district.

Your loving

HARRIET

[The letter which follows is written on the stationery of the Grand Hotel Beauvau, which proudly offers "Vue splendide sur la mer—ascenseur—éclairage electrique—chauffage central à eau chaude—bains—douches—chambre noir à photographies" (Splendid sea view, elevator, electric light, central hot water heating, baths, douches, photographic dark room).]

Dear Family:

I had a beautiful birthday, 'till I left Agay—how I hated to go! But, everybody did something for me. We had an extra fine lunch—such good chicken and sauce, special—and the ice-cream—chocolate—is a never-to-be-forgotten thing. They each wrote a verse and had a joke on me—they were all cute as could be. Mrs. Stein gave me a promise of something she has for me in Paris—also Harriet—so really, my presents are so far all promises. But even the maids helped, by decorating the table! I took my last swim in one of Allan's suits, cause mine was packed, and you should have seen me. Harriet wore one of Mrs. Stein's, and Theresa wore one of hers, too. We were an awful looking crowd. But I don't care, I can almost dive now—made a couple of rather good ones the last morning, but I shall have to practice a bit more before perfection will be reached.

We drove to San Raphael in the carriage, and took the train from there. We arrived here at about half past seven—driving up in an auto bus that went at the rate of an hundred miles a minute—the streets were so crowded, there was such hustle and bustle that we almost perished. We came here and washed and then started out for a restaurant that is famous in the Baedecker—on the port. We went into a dirty little place—everything was awful, the "types" passing up and down gave me the jim jams—finally, we didn't finish—just had tomatos and fish, and went over to a respectable street where we sat outside a café and had hot chocolate. It was so hot and there were so many people—all classes—so many poverty-stricken faces, that we could stand it no longer, so all drifted back here to bed. Our rooms face the port, so after all was quiet last night, I stood by the window a while and all I could see being drunken men, decided to go to bed. I had no sooner gotten comfortable trying to compose my poor head enough to calm down a bit before going to sleep, when I heard a "meow"— and, jumping up in bed, saw a huge black cat coming in my window. I got up, shooed him away, but he wouldn't stay away, so I closed the shutters and went to sleep without air—but, when I remember having slept seven straight hours, without even turning over, I don't think I have much to say.

Well, Theresa and Rachael went on to Paris this morning, and Harriet and I went "sightseeing." We walked along the port—of all the awful odors!! We wandered into a place—a kind of stock-exchange—where the women who sell the fish on the street buy it. They were all running around with fish and screaming prices etc. until I wondered what I had to see next, when I turned around and saw an eel wiggling toward me. I ran! We took the suspension ferry across the bay—It was very nice—We walked some more on the other side, then took a car and went up on the funicular to the church on the hill—famous old church of centuries ago—noted now for the fine view one can get from there. It was misty this morning. We came down again and went into the café we should have been in but missed last night—for a drink of water—it was very good! We came back here for a rest, and had lunch here in the hotel. It was so wonderfully genteel and quiet!

Harriet is resting now, and I am resting mentally cause I know that she is finished with sightseeing for this time at least.

125

I almost forgot—I saw a drunken negro sailor this morning, with an American flag for a neck-tie. I wanted to weep at the disgrace—but I didn't. We had planned going to Monte Cristo's island this afternoon, but its too hot to move, and really, I have an impression of one of the biggest ports in the world that will last me a life-time! We go on to Paris in the morning—our apartment will be ready for us. Agay is the most perfect spot in the world.

Lots of love,

Sis

31 Rue de Vaugirard, Paris, Sept. 5, 1913.

Dear Family:

I felt so apologetic after having sent that letter from Marseilles that I wanted to run after it and haul it back. I wrote it just after lunch, and it was such a desperately hot day, and everything seemed too terrible to look at—but, when Harriet woke up at about two, and we asked the clerk to tell us a cool place to go, and he sent us to a café where we sat until about four thirty, and ate such cold coffee ice-cream—things commenced to look a bit different. When we left the café we took the famous drive around the town, and along the sea shore, and it was glorious. The cocher was especially nice, and took us all kinds of pretty view places. Then when we got to the Palace of the Princess Eugenie and saw the port down below, and the church way up on the hill—it was a never-to-be-forgotten picture! It was without doubt the most beautiful scene I have ever seen. We drove until seven—saw thousands of people swimming—everyone trying to keep cool—but by that time, the air had become soft and velvety. I am so glad we stayed over even though the first night and next morning were the most awful I have ever experienced. We took dinner at the hotel—and afterward went to a café for black coffee. We went to the same one as we had been to in the afternoon, and it was so pleasant, we stayed there until nine, and then home to bed.

We had our reservations for seats next the windows in our compartement, and were most comfortably established until we got to Lyons. I don't mean that it was comfortable—cause it was too hot—but at Lyons an enormous woman, her husband and daughter came in. They were of the peasant type—so nice and gentle and sweet—but so horribly dirty! Harriet and I went into the corridor for a while, and when we came back, we found the windows closed and you could have cut the air with a knife! I boldly opened both windows wide, and the place aired almost immediately, thank Heavens! It was raining by then. So we were once more comfortable—at least I was—Harriet stayed in the corridor. I sat on my seat next the open window while we passed through such beautiful country, and I couldn't stand having the old woman stand looking out the window, so I asked her if she would take my seat. She was delighted and thanked me most heartily—told me they had been travelling four days—from Tunis—had had little sleep, and were worn out. They told me also that they expected to see many wonderful things in Paris. One thing the old lady was most excited about was going to the opera—she hoped some of the big artists would be here now—I almost dropped!

Then she asked me where I was from and I

told them America. Oh! she said, "Il y a beaucoup d'argent en Amerique." She asked me if the country in America was as pretty as that through which we were passing!! I told them, also, how long it took to make the trip, and it almost finished all three of them. They had been travelling so long, they thought. Finally, they got their lunch basket out, and invited me to take dinner with them. I refused, however, and went into the dining car. When we came back, the light was out, and all three were stretched out asleep. We stayed in the corridor until we landed in Paris, at half past ten.

Laurie and Sallie were here waiting for us. The apartment is so clean and fresh—it is delightful to be in it again. The concierge beams on me as if I were his long lost daughter. And, at nine this morning, the new maid walked in and took possession. She had been engaged by the proprietaire for us. All I had to do was prepare the breakfast, and the concierge even did the shopping for that.

I have reams to do now, and am just about written out. Loads of love—thanks, everybody, for the nice birthday wishes—they made me feel so good!!

Sis

[The next letter is from Harriet to her mother.]

31 Rue de Vaugirard, September 9

Dear Grandma—

We had such a busy time yesterday afternoon. First we went down to our bank and found much excitement. The bank was that day changing hands, having been absorbed by a big English bank. They told me that the new firm would not cash checks on American banks—but the paying teller gave me a note to another bank in which he is to have a position next week—and I went there and had a check cashed. The old bank told me that they would continue to forward my mail—but you had better send it to this address.

Then we went to the American consul to ask about duty. I had hoped to return on the basis of my old residence in Paris—counting my 2 years in America as a visit—but the consul said that he did not think that that basis would be accepted. He said that if we remained here the full year however that we could both go in without duty—on any articles intended for our selves.

As the duty is an important factor, we have concluded to remain here two weeks longer. That will bring us to the beginning of November. We shall take passage on one of the quick boats that leave then. The Kaiser Wilhelm II—on which I came over with Alice leaves on Nov. 5—and the Olympia— also a six day boat—about that time.

We marched all around town yesterday, Sylvia holding on to her Lehnhardt's candy as if it were rubies.

We saw the Strausses off on Sunday morning. The little baby looked rosy and happy, as if all places were alike to him. Mr. Strauss promised to call upon you when he went to Oakland. He will be a great success at home—for his voice is splendid. He studied here with De Retzke [*de Reszke*]—and his voice improved wonderfully.

Paris is full of Americans on their return towards America. This afternoon we are going up the river to St. Cloud—and walk. Tomorrow—we are going to Chantilly—and next week we are going to see the chateaux in the Lorraine. We seem so brown next to everybody. I didn't realize how burnt we were until we got into our city clothes. Alice and Gertrude are spending the weeks in Spain. Theresa has moved to the Girls' Club. She is installing a piano in her room and expects to practice and give lessons. Strangely enough, the American teachers here are paid as highly as they are at home. We have a friend—a pupil of Bauer—who received $4 an hour here last spring.

Did I write you how interesting it was at Marseilles? Our hotel was right on the port, and ships came and went all day. We spent a day and two nights there. In the morning we went to the market hall—where hundreds of rolly-poly fish women went bidding for fish. It sounded like the roar of a stock exchange. The odor of the fish was too much for Sylvia—and a great eel on the floor—coiled with his head up like the serpent in the garden of Eden—frightened her so that she ran out of the place.

There is one street in Marseilles famous for the life. There are cafes from one end to the other— and the sidewalks are lined with people eating and drinking at little tables. We drove along the sea and around the town—and saw hundreds of men and women bathing in the different establishments—entrance varying from ten to two cents. The view of the ports and the city was magnificent from the Pharo—an old palace that used to belong to the Empress Eugenie.

It was a long hot trip back to Paris from Marseilles—13 hours. Fortunately it rained the last eight hours. We got into Paris at ten at night, and were glad to find the Strausses to welcome us into our house.

I must tell you about last evening. I was walking alone when a man walked up to me and said "Petite—vous êtes belle." Little one, you are beautiful. I said "Not enough to hurt you." Wasn't that funny?

Tell Robert that we received the letter with the records—thank you, Babe. Love to the family and Mrs. Peabody and a great deal to your own self from

Your loving

HARRIET

31 Rue de Vaugirard, Sept. 11, '13

Dear Family:

Paris is beautiful! I knew it before but I know it more now—September is the month—everyone always says so, and everyone is always right. This morning it was too cold to stay home without a fire, so Harriet and I left the house at nine o'clock and went out to the Bois—driving thro the streets was lovely! At the Bois we got out, and walked along by the bridle-path—it was glorious! and such horses— I have never seen such horses and such riders. From ten to twelve is the "chic" time there—all the very nicest people in Paris come out and ride, or come in their cars and then walk. It is especially pleasant because all the people are the really nice, gentle kind. It was so beautiful—just nice air for walking, and we really had a superb morning, coming back at half-past twelve.

Yesterday afternoon Rachel and Harriet and I went across town to see what we could see—which finished with being nothing for us, but a dress and coat at the model-shop for Rachel. I have stopped now, for myself, as I have all I need, except perhaps some underwear, and a coat for the steamer, which I shall be glad to have for the automobile when I get home. I am not going to get one too heavy for the street, however.

It just came to me, that I have never thanked the boys for the candy. You don't know how it is having it here, all the way from Lehnhardt's, and so fresh. There was a friend in to dinner Tuesday night, who almost lost all control when she saw the name on the box—she is from S.F. I gave some to the concierges last night, and when I told them it was from America they handled it as though it were a gold mine.

Tonight Gene Oliver is coming in to dinner. She is a young girl from S.F., studying drawing of some sort. This afternoon we are going to Mrs. de Buyko's to tea, and tomorrow night Mildred Aldrich is coming to dinner. Saturday night we are going to Coopers to dinner, and Sunday the Norledges are coming in here—so, we are getting to be real sociable! Next week we expect to go to the Chateau district—it is a trip of about five days. We are really going this time, cause we don't want to wait 'till its too late in the season. Winter seems to be hurrying itself a bit.

I must tell you how I had my umbrella covered for six francs! with even better material than I had on it before. Isn't that marvellous?

First week in November still holds good for sailing, so far as we know now. But every time we go out for information we get it altogether different than the time before. I mean on the subject of customs—cause that is really what is making us stay so long here. However, the Herold has issued a pamphlet on customs which I shall procure today, and maybe we'll get straightened out.

Just so very much love to everybody,

Sis

[Harriet's letter to Jeffrey, which follows, was written the following day.]

September 12

Dear Jeffrey:

There is some mistake somewhere, or else I wrote so concentrated that it sounded authoritative. I must put a few hours between the time I screw up my mind for clear thinking—and my putting my thinking on paper, if the result is so bad.

You must know that all I wanted to say was that it would be foolish to make your father incur great expense (he said that a house would cost him at least $30,000) and displace your mother against her will—on account of Sylvia. What I had in mind was to relieve you from the necessity of making a violent change because of Sylvia—who at the worst (staying next door) was quite able to weather the situation—difficult though it might be.

Of course I realized that it would be painful for the boy, but I did not think that even that was sufficient reason for moving.

If, however, it is not because of Sylvia—but for social & business reasons that are obvious to you all—why not? I never have dreamed of interfering or indeed of having any contrary opinion—particularly as the neighborhood has always been unpleasant to me.

We are off to the Louvre for a change—so good-bye.

Love to the family from

HARRIET

31 Rue de Vaugirard, September 15, '13

Dear Family:

I'll begin it now, in the good old way, and finish it for mail time tomorrow. I received a card from Albert, from Berlin. He did splendid work over here with Bauer, and is now going to spend the winter in Berlin.

We got our furs back from storage this morning—Mine are so beautiful—you will love them, Mama—just what you always wanted me to have—beautiful big white fluffy things—I never knew they were so pretty.

Yesterday, Mrs. Edna Aiken, Harriet's friend from San Francisco, came in to tea. She is nice as can be, travelling like mad, trying to see the world. (Harriet says she's travelling exceptionally quietly.) She has her little boy, and German maid. If you know anyone who would like to have a German maid who knows all about children, and being a ladies maid, and is learning English and wants to go to America, and, if this person will take her on a guarantee of her staying with them a year, and will pay her passage over, and give her very little wages for the first year, Mrs. Aiken will bring her to them.

The other day I heard that my nice little French teacher had died this summer. I was so sorry, cause I really was fond of her. But I knew, before we went away, that she was terribly sick.

We spent the afternoon at the Louvre the other day, and I loved it so. I think if I stayed here about twenty years I might almost begin to appreciate Paris. It is so wonderful now, when it isn't raining. We took a long walk in the Bois the other day, and it is lovely—we go out there so often.

While I think of it, I want to tell you what I did down at the Gallerie Lafayette the other day. I saw a woman pass me and she looked strangely familiar, I couldn't take my eyes off her. So I listened to her when she talked to the sales girl to see if she were talking English. Well, she was, but still I couldn't get up enough courage to speak to her. Finally she went, and I ran after her, grabbed her by the arm, and said, "Aren't you from Oakland, California." She said "yes"—looked scared because she didn't recognize me. Finally I said "You know Mrs. Salinger, don't you?" Well, she embraced me on the spot, ran with me to her friends, whom I don't know, and got so excited I felt I had really done something. She was a Mrs. Jacobs, I think, but anyhow, you know, Mama, the one who was at Van Rosens in Los Gatos with her husband, who has since died—Also, they always sat in the Synagogue one row in front of us to the left. Now you know, don't you? She said she sails next month and is going to see you when she gets home. She looked about ten years younger—and—I am so glad I spoke to her.

Last night I stopped to call on Miss Lewis and her brother, who have been to the Chateau District lately, and who had volunteered some information. They are very nice—from some part of the south of the States. The man just finished college and is over studying art and his sister is keeping him company. We are going to the Chateau District tomorrow instead of today—cause Mrs. Aiken is coming in to lunch and wont be in Paris long enough for Harriet to see her when we return.

Mama dear, your letter in answer to mine, made me so happy—even too happy to cry, as I usually do at your letters. I am so glad, so very glad to be coming home to everybody!

Lots of love,

Sis

31 Rue de Vaugirard—Paris, September 23

Dear Family:

Rachel is coming in in a minute to go across town shopping, but I'll write a few lines, anyhow. Yesterday afternoon we had such a wonderful time. Harriet and Mrs. Aiken and I went out to Matisses place. He has some new things and we wanted to see them. Mr. Matisse and Mrs. Matisse entertained us, had tea for us, etc. They are such lovely people—and their grounds are so beautiful and so beautifully kept. The daughter of the Matisses is home now, its the first time I've met her, cause she is always off at school in Moroco, but this is her vacation. I couldn't understand her French, and she speaks no other languages, but we really got along very nicely, considering. They have a pet monkey that is adorable. He walked into the place one day, just kind of from nowhere, and has stayed ever since. They have a lot of horses, but I forgot to enquire about them so didn't see them. Mr. Matisse is a swimming enthusiast so we had a fine time talking about diving and strokes and things. And, the youngest boy, who used to paint from morning 'till night, has suddenly taken to writing. They gave us something of his, it is prose, sort of Impression work, and is really remarkably good. He is eleven, I believe. I could go on talking about that family for hours, it seems so funny, when I think that you probably aren't in the least interested. *[Among the facts omitted by Sylvia because of their lack of interest is that on one of these visits Matisse produced a sketch of Harriet (see plate 14). According to Sylvia, he was at first quite reluctant, because he didn't enjoy portraiture; he finally agreed to do the sketch when Harriet offered him $100.]*

I got tired of writing about the Chateau district—that's why I almost didn't mention it this time. The weather stays just the same kind of uncertain, with showers every once in a while, so it would be useless to go until it clears. *[And now Harriet takes over.]*

Sylvia has gone in to dress, leaving me to finish her letter. It's discouraging about the chateaux trip—it is a trip for sunshine and the sunshine wont come. But we still hope.

My present interest is to get something to wear. I have literally nothing—and there are a few clothes that I must get. So we are all three off now. I fear that Sylvia will have to pay duty—It seems that the question asked is "Where is your home."

We haven't engaged our steamer yet, but it is

still the first week in September. *[Sylvia crosses out* September *and inserts* November.*]*

I'll write a real letter for the next mail. So good-bye for the present.

Lovingly,

HARRIET

31 Rue de Vaugirard, Sept. 30

Dear Family:

Pearl Cooper just left, and while waiting for lunch I shall start this. She told us her husband has started out the season with five pupils. He is very young and a pupil of Bauer.

I have started work on pitch again—with Theresa. I take a lesson of a half hour every morning. Every time I think of not being able to sing for you when I get home, I could cry—but it won't be more than a few weeks before I will.

The other day, when I took my walk in the Luxembourg gardens, I heard a terrific noise, and looking up saw a Zeppelin right over my head—it was flying so low it just escaped the roofs, and it was so tremendous it scared the life out of me. There is nothing unusual about seeing an air-ship around here at all, but every time I see one it thrills me. Yesterday afternoon we were riding out in the country and one flew over us. Then the day before I was up on top of the Arc de Triomphe and could see one flying way off in the distance. The view of Paris from the Arc is the most beautiful thing you could imagine. It was a very clear day, and we walked over from here, then climbed up, and it took my breath away—the magnificence of it. You know that is where the fifteen boulevards meet—and it looked as if they were starting there and reaching out to the ends of the world.

Then, riding out at Robinson yesterday was lovely—The trees are beginning to shed, so the roads are covered with leaves—such beautiful coloring everywhere. Sunday afternoon we went up the river to investigate a swimming place someone told us of. We went on one of the little river steamers that run along so smoothly and quick as lightning. It was a beautiful trip—the first time I have been in that direction—but we found the water too cold at this time of the year—no one was swimming at all. The whole of Paris, it seemed to me, was out there—such mobs, everybody happy and having such a sort of gentle good time.

We got a letter from Jimmy. He said there will be no Chalmers runabout—That was a blow—but so long as you keep the car for a little run now and then—it is enough for me.

Loads of love,

Sis

October 7, 1913

Dear Family:

Harriet just said to tell you that we haven't our passage yet, so are not sure of our sailing date but still consider the first week in November as the probable time. They tell us everywhere that we can have most any boat we want, and just about the whole of it, so we shall probably get passage a few days before sailing.

Otherwise everything is going swimmingly. I have all my clothes, and such lovely ones—Mama, at last I think that you will approve of the way I look. I adore everything I have, and so will all of you. Harriet ordered a coat yesterday, mole color. It is going to be beautiful! We are waiting for the dressmaker to alter a dress of Harriets after which episode we are going across town to buy Harriet a hat.

In the meantime Paris is so beautiful! The Luxembourg gardens are marvellous, except that they are beginning to fade just a bit now.

Mme. Homolacs just came in and I have been talking a blue streak of French, but Harriet is here now, so I can write. They are doing a regular Alphonse and Gaston stunt about something or other and it is so funny. *[Nina Alexandrowicz-Homolacs was the author-illustrator of a series of books about a shaggy French poodle named Foufou.]*

We went to Versailles last Sunday to see the fountains play. They only play on Sunday during the summer months, and last Sunday was the last time—there were mobs and mobs of people there and the waters were so beautiful. Everywhere you looked you saw a stream shooting up in the air— there are two of them hidden in the forest—that are as high as the trees. We stayed until they turned them off, and just sat around looking. It was especially wonderful that day because there was such a lovely clouded sky.

The dressmaker came, so Harriet has disappeared again, but our guest is looking at prints, so all is well.

Doesn't it seem wonderful to think that in a month from now I shall probably be sailing homeward? How I do want to be home with all of you!

The difficulties are just a bit too much for me, so I think I shall stop trying to write.

Loads of love to everybody,

Sis

31 Rue de Vaugirard, Paris, October 7, 1913

Dearest Ruthie:

I am so crazy about my clothes that I can't wait for you to see them all. Everything is ready except that my coat hasn't come home yet. It is beautiful—with big fur collar and cuffs, and I have an adorable hat the color of the fur—Siberian mole is the fur, do you know it? Kind of gray and white, very soft. I have a rose colored velvet evening dress that is a marvel. I ought to look like a Turkish princess in it. I wore it the other night at an exhibition and no-body saw any pictures! Everything I have is so beautiful—the girls all laugh at me for adoring my things so. Each time I buy anything new they all ask me if I like it—and never wait for the answer.

Loads of love,

Sis

31 Rue de Vaugirard, Paris, October 23, 1913

Dearest Ruthie:

It is time for dejeuner, but that doesn't matter, cause it ain't ready yet. So, I'll start this anyhow.

We are planning now to get home some time before Thanksgiving, but of course, aren't sure. I hate like anything to leave Paris, and, incidentally, all my very good friends here, but my love for my family is great enough to overbalance it so far. I heard from Mother yesterday and she seems to be so much better—I try to read between the lines to know if she really is improving, and this time was quite satisfied that it is true. I can't wait to get home to her—just to show you all how very much nicer I am.

Tonight Mr. and Mrs. Matisse are coming in to dinner. I am going to practice up on my French so I shall know something of what they are talking about. They are so very, very nice—and they felt really badly when we told them we are going home—We felt so flattered. *[In later years Sylvia often repeated her favorite anecdote about Matisse. He had been observing her at a display of paintings; everyone else was screwing up his or her eyes, or moving in close to check the brushstrokes, or holding up an index finger at arm's length, while Sylvia simply stood there—and looked at the paintings. Finally he approached and offered her a compliment. "Mademoiselle," he said, "you are the only one here who knows how to look at art."]*

That's about all I can think of now, but I'll leave this open, anyhow 'till tomorrow—mail day.

Tomorrow

We have about decided to sail on the Geo. Washington on the sixteenth of November—aren't taking passage yet cause at this time of the year it is better to wait till the last minute. Harriet is going to add a line, so—

Lots of love to the happy family,

Sis

[Harriet adds several lines.]

Dear Ruth:

Unless something unforseen happens we shall sail on the 16th of November, stop a day in New York—and then straight for home.

We are pretty busy these days, getting ready to return. After many attempts, I secured two lovely dresses that brought me much rest and comfort. I can now hope to grace your home.

The Matisses were in to dinner last night, and we had a beautiful time. Matisse is a delightful story teller and his imitations of people are so good. They brought us a great mass of colored dahlias from their garden in the environs of Paris—and our salon is quite resplendent this morning. I am so fond of both of them.

Miss Miller leaves tomorrow. I met her this morning—red-eyed—because she was leaving Sarah, whom she loves.

Sylvia is clamoring for me to finish—so good-bye—and no end of love to you all from

Your own

HARRIET

October 28, 1913

Dear Family:

I met a man yesterday who is going to sail on the Geo Washington on the sixteenth and he told me the agent said they were receiving a great many demands for November—so—I guess we'll go down tomorrow or today to engage passage. It is a seven day boat, so we land in New York on the 23rd about and probably leave the next day, reaching home! the twenty-ninth or thirtieth. Does not it sound close? It does to me.

Life has been most awful strenuous of late, for one who is accustomed to the simple quiet life. Yesterday I went to lunch with the Kohlbergs to an Italian Restaurant—after which we went up the Eiffel Tower—It was a beautiful day and the view is extraordinary—then we went to the Café de la Paix for an ice. Mr. Kohlberg, in answer to my question of "Do you know my father?" answered "Who doesn't?"

We are hearing wonderful things about Laurence Strauss. He has the position of first tenor in the Trinity Church in S.F.—the highest position a singer can have in S.F. *[For the rest of his life he remained in the Bay Area, teaching in San Francisco and Berkeley and singing in recitals and in Christian Science churches. Sylvia's mother always maintained that Laurence Strauss would have had a great career if he hadn't been so short.]*

Sunday afternoon we went to the automobile show. I have never seen such a thing anywhere. The cars are beautiful and almost without number.

Saturday we went up the river to Charenton— a ride of three quarters of an hour—for three sous. We walked for a long time along the canal, and on the shore of a beautiful little river that runs into the Seine. The woods are lovely—all the trees are covered with the autumn-colored leaves. *[And that, except for a fragment appended to this letter by Harriet, is the end of the letters from France. The rest of this letter— and any letters that might have followed—are missing. Shortly before her death in 1950, Harriet borrowed the letters from Sylvia, to help her in a never-to-be-completed book she was writing about post-impressionist pre-war Paris; this may explain the missing letters.]*

Letterhead of the Hotel Knickerbocker, New York City
Sylvia and Harriet stayed at the Knickerbocker for several days
before boarding the *Amerika* for France.

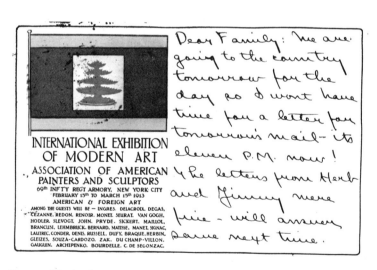

Postcard from the Armory Show, New York City
The International Exhibition of Modern Art, held February 15–
March 15, 1913, introduced post-impressionism to a startled United
States.

TÉLÉPHONE 735·46
744·87 - 744·88

ADRESSE TÉLÉGRA^{que}
LUTETIAOTEL-PARIS

SQUARE
DU BON MARCHÉ

HOTEL LUTETIA

43, BOUL^D RASPAIL
PARIS

PARIS, le **Nov. 4** 191 **2**.

Dear Family:

We just got some letters - one from Lena, one from Herb, which was a corker, and one from Ruth. Also, one from Phyllis which was so much about you all that I feel as if it was from you too. The details of Herb's trip were wonderful! Harriet says, "I love the way he met all those nice people after he left us." But, anyhow, I am glad the trip turned out to be such a very pleasant one. I have not received the pictures you sent, Herbie, but always have hopes. The ones I took were not worth sending.

Letter from the Hotel Lutetia, Paris
Sylvia and Harriet stayed at the Lutetia during October and November 1912.

Sylvia Salinger, 31 rue de Vaugirard, Paris, February 1913

Harriet Levy, Sarah Stein, and Sylvia Salinger, 31 rue de Vaugirard, February 1913
Sylvia is in her beloved and often-mentioned white fox furs.

The Stein family, c. 1905
Left to right: Leo Stein, Allan Stein, Gertrude Stein, Therese Ehrman, Sarah Stein, Michael Stein. This photograph was taken several years before Sylvia's arrival in Paris.

Harriet Levy (*left*) and Alice B. Toklas, 1907
This photograph was probably taken at Fiesole.

Gertrude Stein's salon, 27 rue de Fleurus
This photograph, taken at the time of Sylvia's visit, clearly
shows the famous Picasso portrait of Gertrude.

**Exterior of Michael and Sarah Stein's home, a converted
church, 58 rue Madame**

Michael and Sarah Stein's dining room, 58 rue Madame

"The Girl with Green Eyes" (over the sideboard) was painted by Matisse in 1909 and later purchased by Harriet Levy. It now hangs in the San Francisco Museum of Modern Art.

Michael and Sarah Stein's salon, 58 rue Madame (view no. 1)

Michael and Sarah Stein's salon (view no. 2)

Michael and Sarah Stein's salon (view no. 3)

Sketch of Harriet Levy by Henri Matisse

Michael Stein, Max Rosenberg, Sylvia Salinger, and Allan Stein on horseback at Robinson

Corniche de Lesterel — La Rade d'Agay et le Grand Hôtel

Postcard from le Grand Hôtel, Agay
"The Group" stayed here from June 24 to September 2, 1913.

"The Group," Agay Bay
Left to right: Allan Stein, Sylvia Salinger, Harriet Levy, Rachel Miller, Therese Ehrman, Sarah Stein.

Sylvia Salinger and Harriet Levy swimming at Agay, 1913

"The Group," Agay
Left to right: Therese Ehrman, Harriet Levy, Sarah Stein, Sylvia Salinger, Rachel Miller, Allan Stein.

AFTERWORD

INDEX

AFTERWORD

Sylvia and Harriet returned to California in late November 1913. Six months later, the Belle Époque ended as, with the assassination of the Austrian archduke Ferdinand at Sarajevo, World War I began.

Harriet continued to travel and to write and to collect art. Her book of reminiscences of Jewish family life in early San Francisco, *920 O'Farrell Street*, was successfully published by Doubleday in 1947. And the paintings and sculpture that she purchased in Europe now form a major part of the collection of the San Francisco Museum of Modern Art.

As for Sylvia, on her way home—both on board the steamer and in a hotel in New York—she experienced the worst of the panic attacks that had plagued her since early adolescence. Back home in California, she did continue to study voice, stopping only when she experienced another attack at her teacher's studio. In 1919, at the age of 30, she married Garry Eaton Bennett, a handsome naval officer whose mother was descended from the younger brother of Thomas Jefferson. Sylvia and Garry had two sons. My brother Dick (originally Garry Jr.) was born in 1920; when I arrived five years later Sylvia insisted that I be named for her father. Early in 1927 Garry Sr. departed from Piedmont (we had been established in a little house across the street from the Salinger mansion); he was never heard from again. Papa Salinger died in 1941; Sylvia's sons grew up and moved away; her mother died in 1956; and Sylvia became a recluse.

For the last few decades of her long life she never left the safety of her beloved home. And she never tired of telling people—with a giggle—what Gertrude Stein had said about her during her one trip abroad: "I don't see what all the fuss is about. Sylvia is just a very pretty girl from the country."

ASB

INDEX

Albert Salinger Bennett studied Dramatic Art at the University of California at Berkeley and received a Master of Fine Arts degree from the Yale Drama School. He served as an assistant to Audrey Wood, the legendary playwrights' agent, and as story editor for Kraft Television Theatre. After spending two decades writing and editing reference books (most prominently at Funk and Wagnalls, where he was editor of the yearbook series), he returned to his first love—acting. He has appeared in numerous off-Broadway and off-off-Broadway productions, television soap operas, feature films, and commercials.